Perfect Escape

An Adventure on Route 66

CHERYL CHURCH

The Perfect Escape An Adventure on Route 66

ISBN – 13:978-1543190816

ISBN – 10: 1543190812

Other Publishing:

The Perfect Escape "The Whimsical and Odd World of Cheryl Church"

Note from the Author:

I have spent many months researching about each state through which the road travels. I have even stepped off the four lanes and onto the two lanes to see what I was missing in our fast-paced society. I have had coffee at some great "mom and pop" operations, eaten a sandwich in a 120-year-old building, driven through a town that once had 30,000 occupants but barely 3,000 today. I have spray-painted on Cadillacs, and most of all I have seen some beautiful country and beautiful people.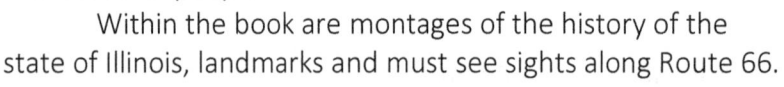

Within the book are montages of the history of the state of Illinois, landmarks and must see sights along Route 66. I have included vintage cars, signs, buildings and a plethora of information.

Many landmarks along the route have changed and even may be gone with only the memories left behind. I have included key facts about Route 66, the development process, and how it affected towns and cities along the route. Route 66 has proven to be the lifeline of America, the vein that the blood runs through freely. Compared to our modern times, the Mother Road's past, though often difficult at times, still seems to be the simpler life. It is my hope that through my artwork you will recognize the significance of the road, how powerful it is to our country and our history.

I enjoy history as well as drawing. When I started the Route 66 coloring book series, I had not planned to add all the history I had just wanted to title pages with interesting facts. But the book grew. I felt that there was such a wonderful story behind not just the road but the ground the road was paved on, I just had to share my findings.

This book is not a historical document but it is my discoveries as I have researched the road for the past 10 months. All the stories that I have written about throughout this unique travel-coloring book were gathered from researching the World Wide Web, or as my husband says, "the internets," visiting with Tourism Bureau's and people that I have met through my adventures on Route 66. I sincerely hope that you enjoy the plethora of information as well as the coloring experience. If you have never traveled Route 66, I would highly recommend it. Each experience I have had has been worth the adventure.

Happy Coloring

This book could not have happened if not for all of the support from my family, friends and colleagues as well as the people I have met along the way of my journey on Route 66, who have shared their memories and especially my husband for always believing in me and being supportive of my many adventures. A special thanks to my cousin Rene Miller Sanchez, without her editorial talents the book would have suffered greatly. My gratitude is forever.

Route 66

The road that no-one forgot!

Route 66 held a special place in Americans' hearts from the beginning. The great road carried us through a new era, a nation on the move. The thousands of stories of hope, heartbreak, love, hate, starting over and dreams of new beginnings linger in the air to this day. They are stories of the past that makeup our great nation, a nation that has been through hard times, war and rebirth.

Route 66 is the most celebrated and famous two-lane road, which fed our culture's love affair with the automobile.

During the 20's the federal highway officials were faced with the growth of automobile ownerships. They needed a better road system that was not disjointed, which caused confusion as Americans began traveling across the country.

The decision to accept "66" as the favored route's designated title was made in Springfield, MO on April 30, 1926, which gave Springfield the right to claim the distinction of "the birthplace of Route 66."

After all the red tape, the road became reality on November 11, 1926. Road signs were erected the following year.

The twentieth century version of the Oregon Trail began, laying its path along old trails from the early explorers and the wagon trains, winding its way westward.

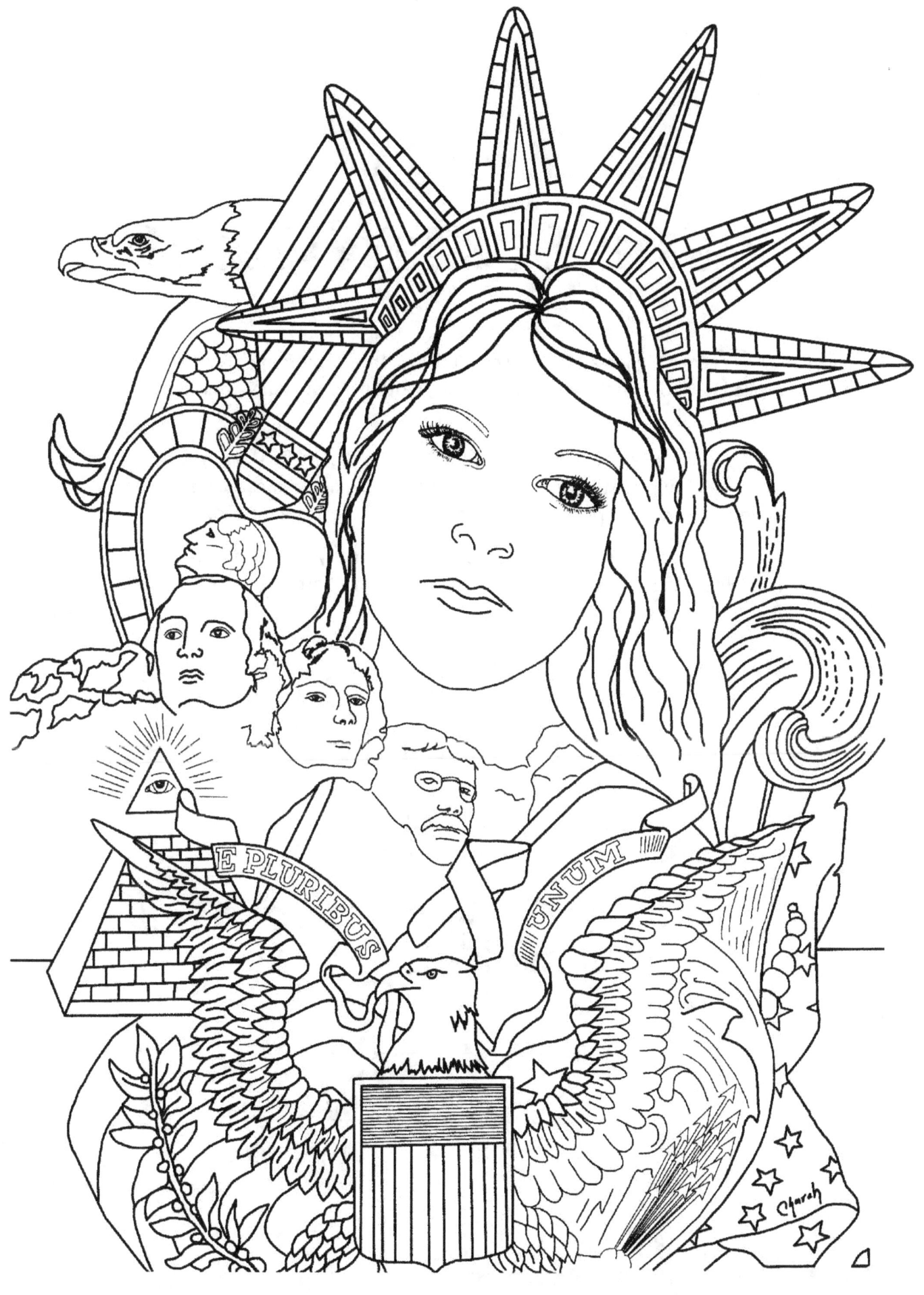

The Golden Road

Across eight states, many counties and three time zones, Route 66 proved to be one of the most memorable, written about and historical roads ever created.

Route 66 was one of the original highways within the U.S. Highway system. Throughout the years, the route acquired many names such as: Will Rogers Highway, the Main Street of America, and the Mother Road.

The Golden Road provided inspiration for many artists and writers, including John Steinbeck, author of "The Grapes of Wrath", who gave Route 66 its best-known name, "The Mother Road."

John
STEINBECK

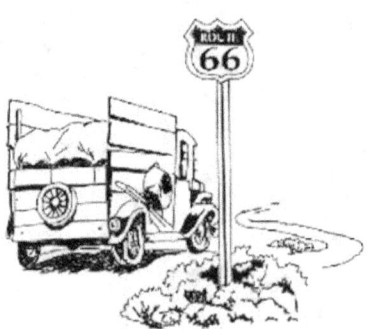

The Grapes
of Wrath

Once you drive part of it - you'll
want to drive all of it!

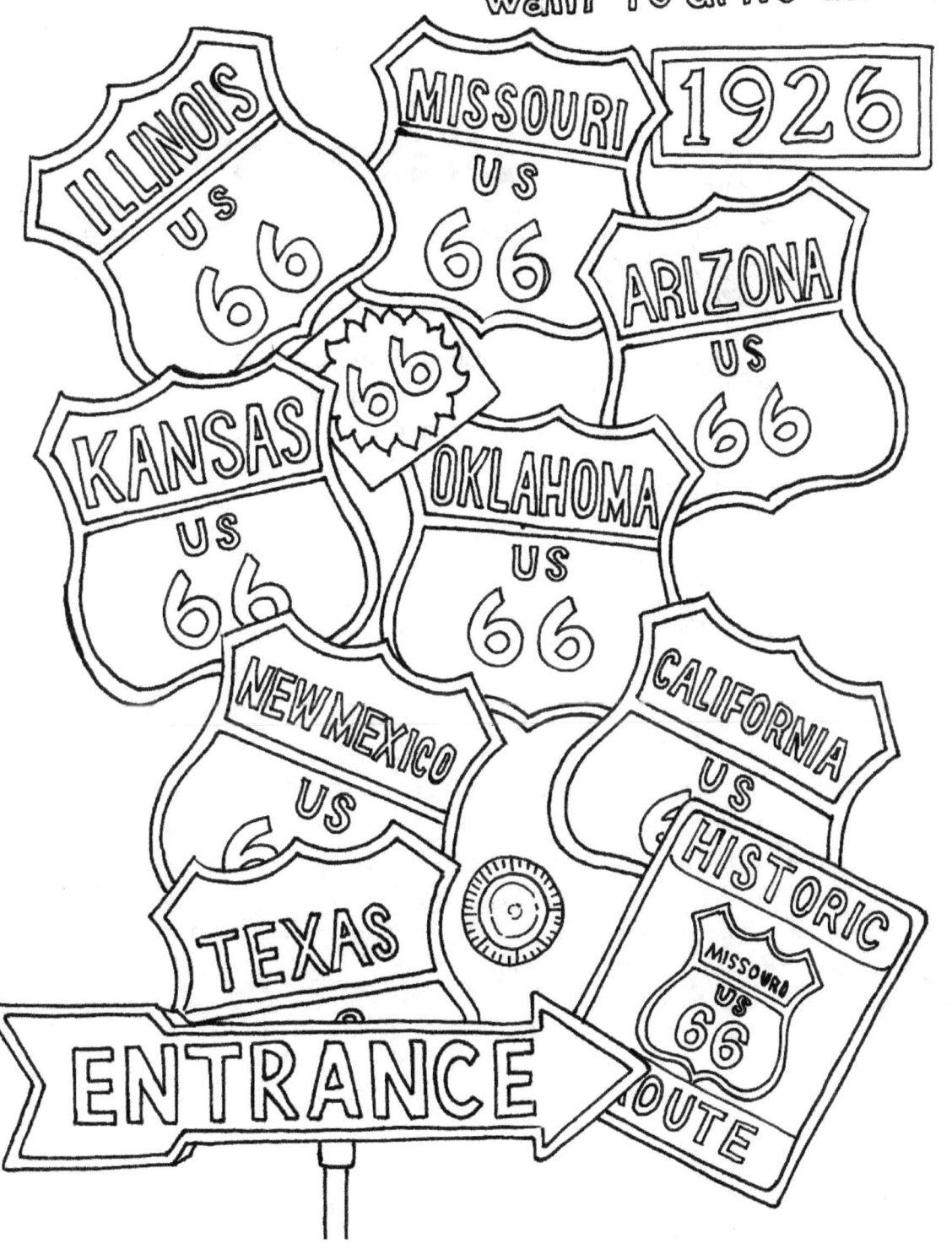

In 1927, the road signs went up for Route 66 across eight states.

Illinois

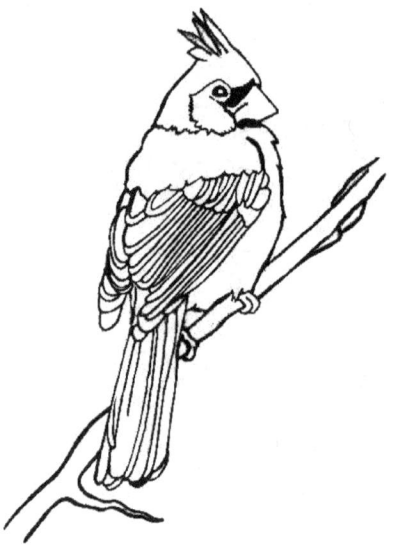

The cardinal symbolizes many things, but to the people of the State of Illinois the cardinal represents their state.

The beautiful State flower is the luscious, vibrant violet.
The great State of Illinois became a part of the Union in 1818.

Three hundred miles of black top ribbon stretches through Illinois. The historical road starts in the Windy City and winds through the state to St. Louis before stretching westward across the country. It all begins at Bow Truss Coffee Roasters, 73 E Jackson Blvd in Chicago.

The numbered highway quickly grew to be the preferred road to the west. The highway was not as old and not as long as some other transcontinental routes. With our nation continuously on the move, Route 66 quickly gained fame as the shortest year-round route between the Midwest and the Pacific coast as it passed through the fabled landscape of the American Southwest. The road transformed the American Wild West from an isolated frontier to an economically vital region of the country, making it possible to connect the cities to the little rural towns.

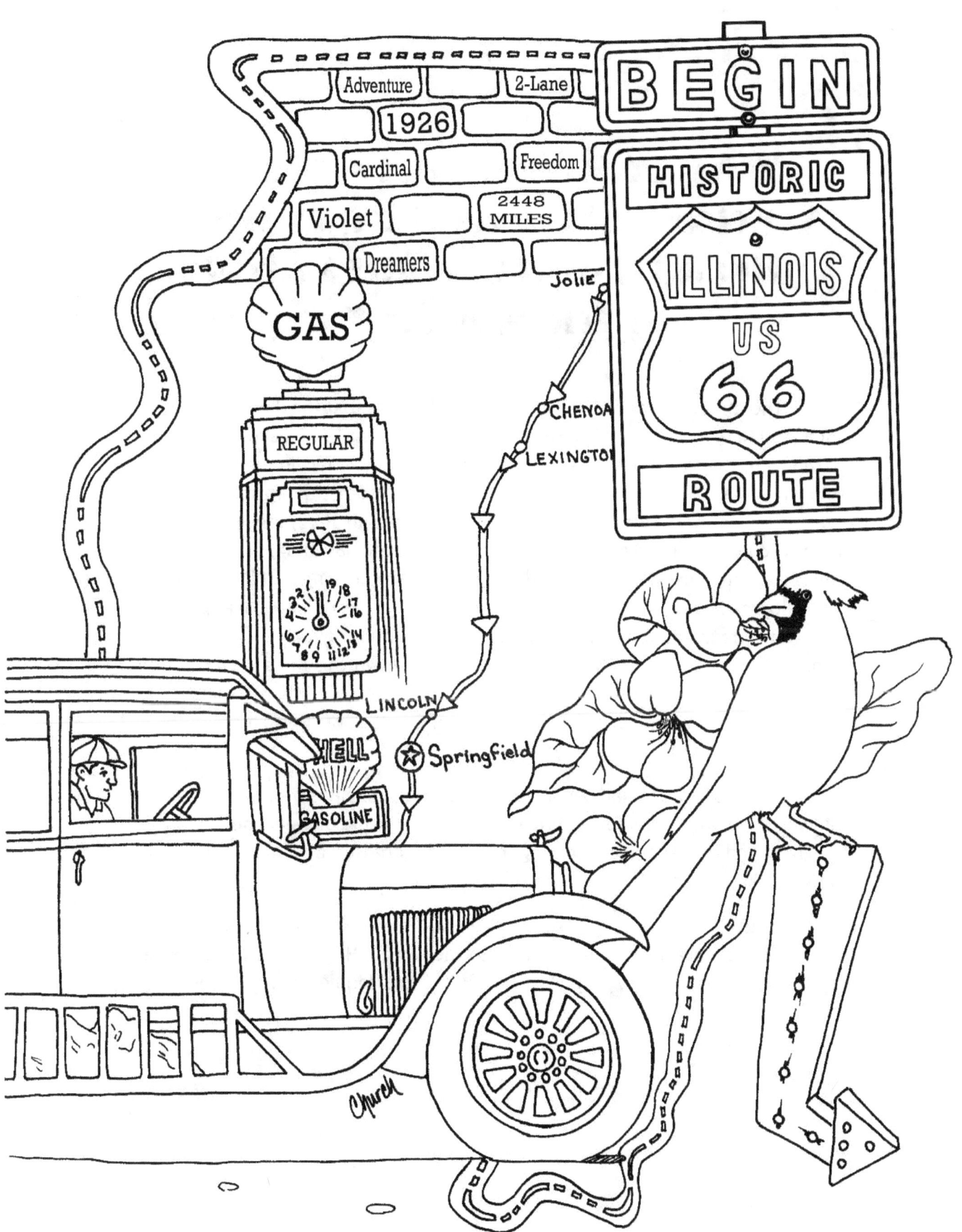

11

"Hog Butcher, Tool Maker, Stacker of Wheat, Player with Railroads, and Freight Handler to the Nation."

The thick roots of sod convinced many farmers that the Illinois land was not a land to be conquered; the treeless plains were just too foreboding. It wasn't until 1840 when farmers began to realize just how fertile the soil was below the sod. The U.S Army built Fort Dearborn to protect the farmers from the Indian uprisings and it was also used as a trading post. In 1812, the Fort was destroyed by Indian raid and took four years to rebuild. By 1832, the Native American resistance ended after the Black Hawk War, leaving Fort Dearborn for redevelopment. The location, along a river and the banks of a lake, was perfect for a water transit hub. As the population rose beyond the fort, it was incorporated as a town in 1833. Naming the new town was not a problem. The wild leeks that grew on the banks of the river, known to the Miami Indians as "chicago," only made it fitting, and the town of Chicago was born. It only took four years for the town of Chicago to become a city.

By 1848 Chicago had become one of the largest cities of the American Midwest. The once small fort that had protected intrepid pioneers now had the telegraph and the railroad, becoming the world's largest grain port with more than 30,000 residents.

In 1916, Carl Sandburg wrote a poem in which he described the speed of the growth of Chicago. In it, he referred to the city as "Hog Butcher, Tool Maker, Stacker of Wheat, Player with Railroads, and Freight Handler to the Nation."

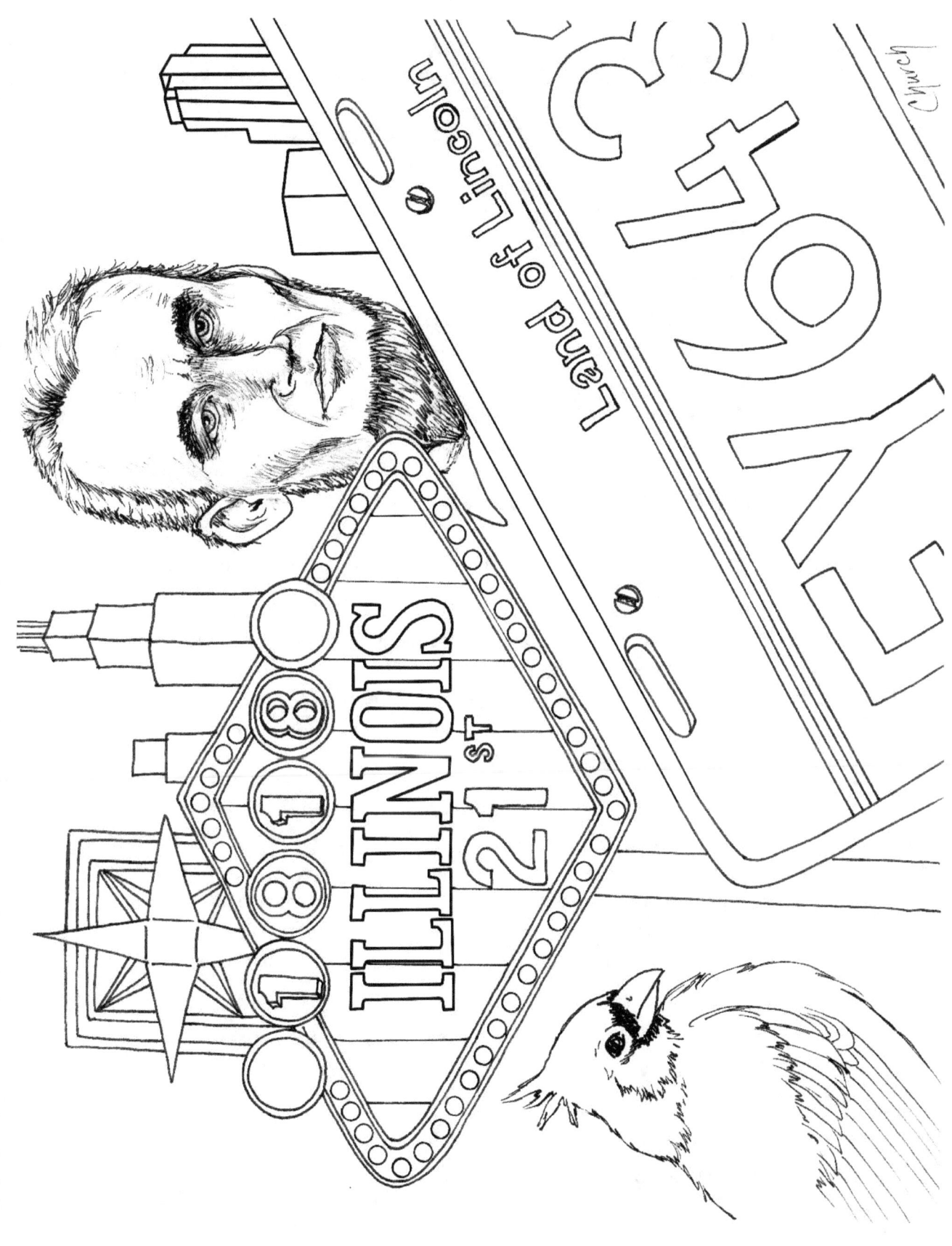

Old Chain of Rocks Bridge
City of Madison

Illinois was the first state to hard surface the highway and the first to replace it with Interstate.

The mighty Mississippi divided the states of Illinois and Missouri, halting the Route 66 continuous road plans. In order to keep the road rolling continuously, the states of Illinois and Missouri had to be connected. The large shoal, or rocky rapids, called the Chain of Rocks created a big challenge for the engineers. Not only did they have to connect the two states but also accommodate the many currents of the river. Bridge construction began on both sides of the river with an estimated cost of $1,250,000 in 1927. The massive 5,353-feet long, 60 feet high and 24 feet wide bridge required a 30-degree turn midway across the water to accommodate the many currents of the Mississippi.

In 1929, ice storms and floods delayed the planned grand opening for New Year's Day. The Chain of Rocks Bridge finally opened to traffic in July of 1929 with a price of $2.5 million, twice the amount initially projected. To offset the extra costs of the bridge a toll of 35 cents per car, with an additional five cents per passenger, was implemented.

As the bridge aged, it began to deteriorate, subsequently forcing its closure in 1970. The unaltered bridge of many years provided the connection between the two states and was an amazing landmark for travelers driving Route 66. The bridge went into limbo for almost 3 decades. The massive iconic creation was abandoned, too expensive to tear down and too narrow and outdated to carry vehicles. The bridge became an eye sore and a place of crime.

Hollywood producers breathed life back into the bridge with the movie *Escape from New York* in 1981. Trailnet struck interest in the bridge, and was excited when the bridge was leased to them in 1998. Trailnet spent four and a half million dollars renovating the bridge so that pedestrians and cyclers could appreciate the great history and beauty.

In 2006 The Chain of Rocks Bridge was listed in the National Register of Historic Places.

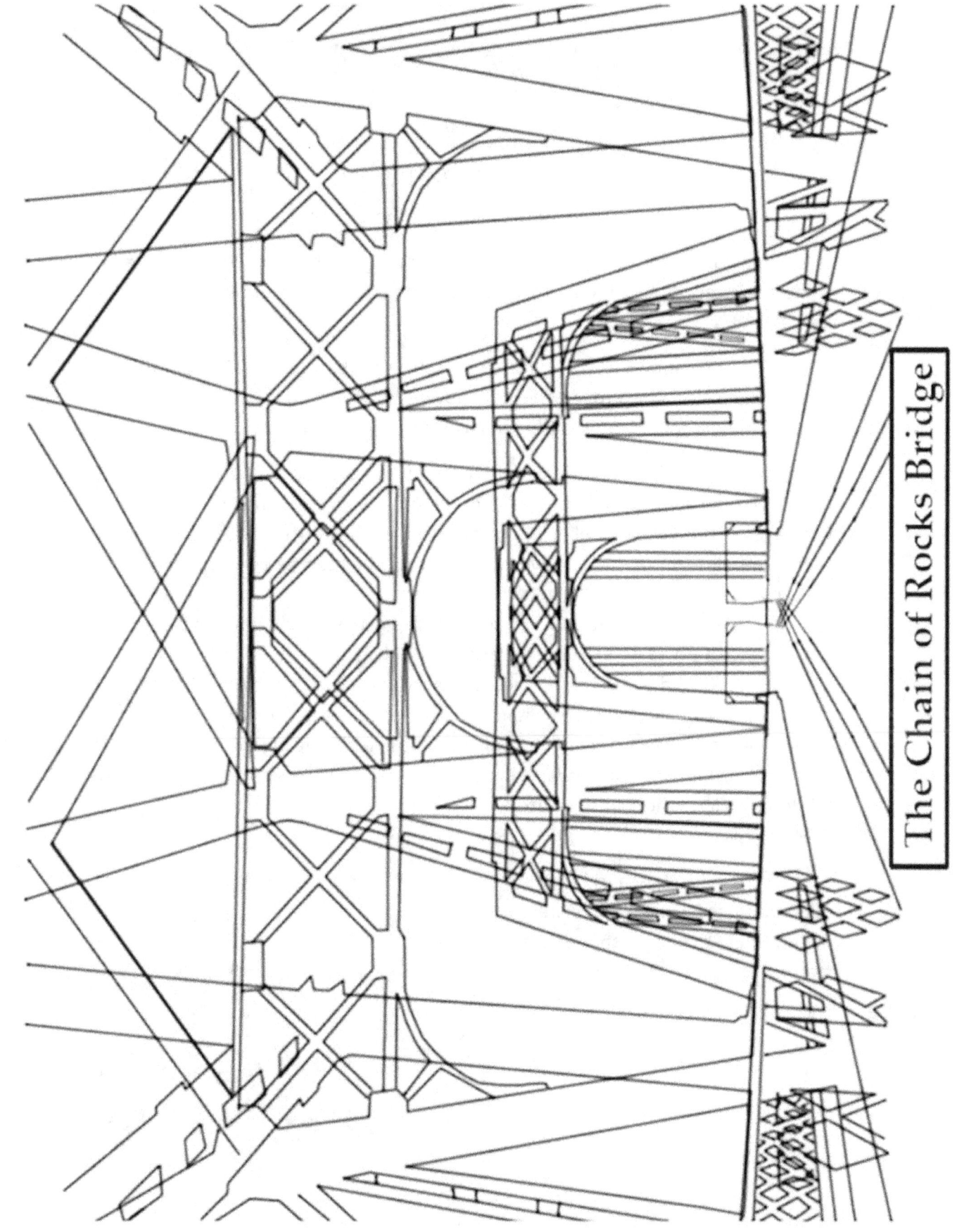

The Chain of Rocks Bridge

Missouri

The Show Me State

Salus populi suprema Lex Esto

"Let the welfare of the people be the supreme law"

Missouri obtained its name from the Missouri Indians that lived along the what is now called the Missouri river. It was established as the 24th state of the Union in 1821.

The captivating Blue bird became Missouri's state bird in 1927 just a year after Route 66 became a road. The state flower, Hawthorn, surrounds the grounds of the capital of Missouri, Jefferson City.

Route 66 travels 333 miles through Missouri, winding through towns such as St. Louis, Willa Ridge, Cuba, Sullivan, Rolla, Arlington, Lebanon, Springfield, Carthage, Webb City and Joplin. Along the way are many attractions that can be seen: St. Louis Arch, Meramec Caverns, George Washington Carver State Park, and Drive Inn Theater in Carthage, MO.

As you cross over the Chain of Rocks Bridge you will glide through the entryway to the Wild, Wild West; the exquisitely elegant Gateway Arch rises from the banks of the Mississippi right in front of your eyes. With the Illinois plains in your rear view mirror, waiting ahead of you, the road will lead to where there are oil wells, cowboys, and the Bible belt. Traveling through bluffs, rolling hills and flat plateaus, Route 66 closely follows the route of a pre-Civil War stage line.

To this day, Missouri has more miles of Route 66 still under state management than any other of the 8 states.

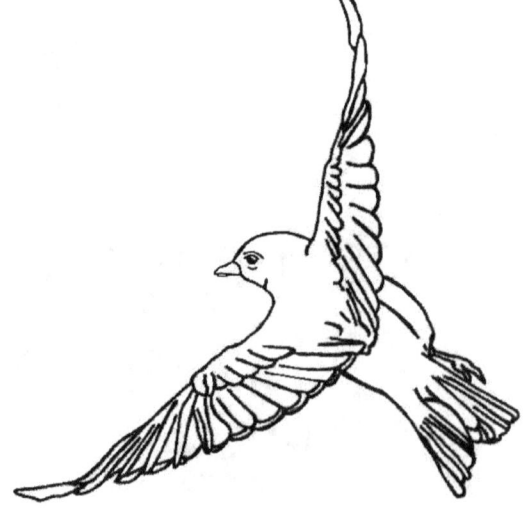

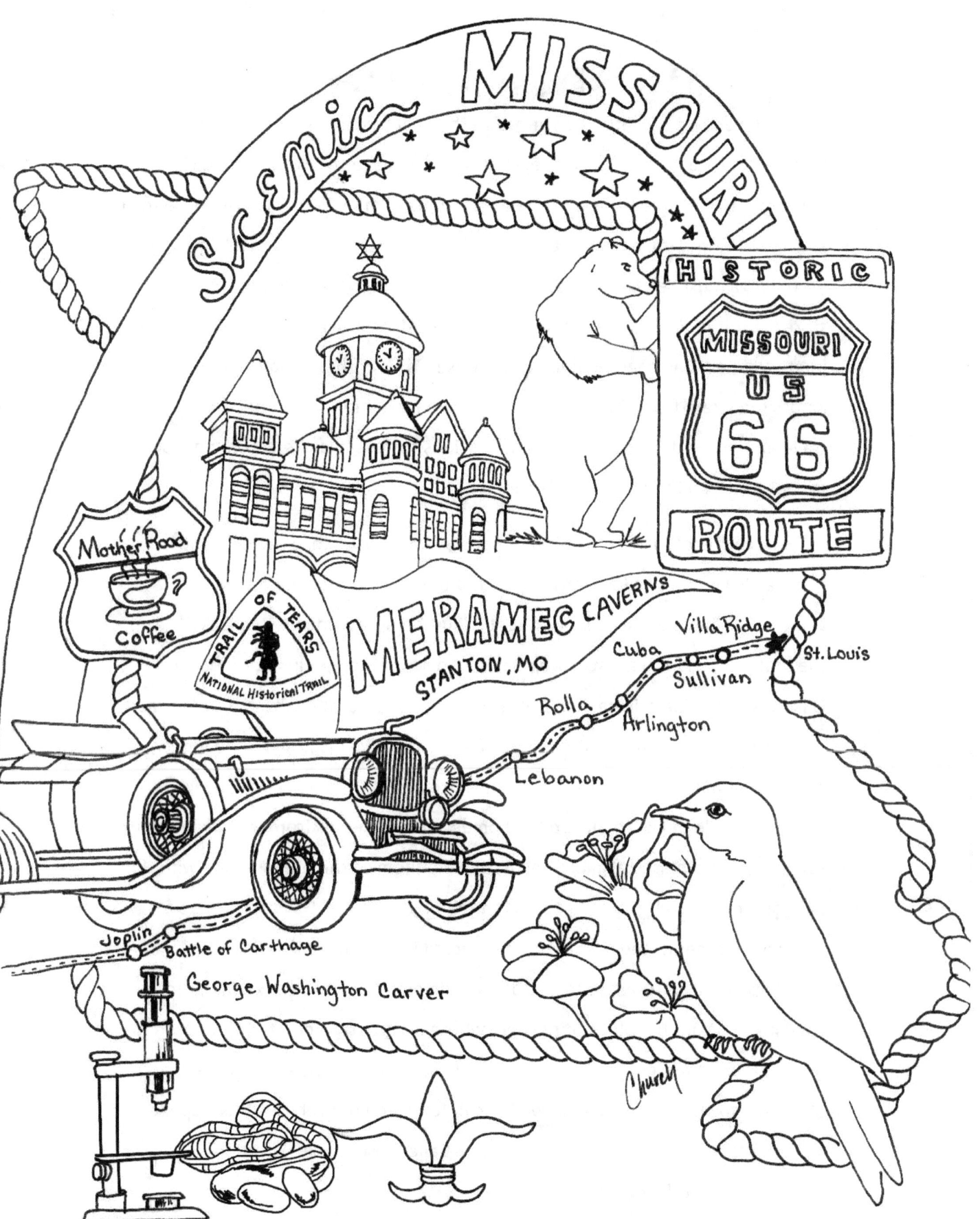

The Show Me State

The Show Me State, the state with the only remaining Drive-In along Route 66, located east of Carthage, Missouri. Carthage, known for the Civil War battlegrounds, Phelps House, Precious Moments Chapel, Power House Museum, and Boots Motel, is a nostalgic town overflowing with character. While in Carthage, a must-see is the beautiful square consisting of a variety of antique stores, a coffee shop, a hardware store, and a deli as well as the amazing, highly photographed, Carthage Marble Court House. The Mother Road Coffee House, across the street from the courthouse, is the hangout for many Route 66 travelers. While drinking a variety of delicious coffees, travelers from near and far put a tack on the map of their hometown.

A couple of miles' northeast of Carthage and just a mile off Route 66 is Red Oak II a vision of a local artist.   It has authentic old buildings, an old cemetery, jailhouse and I cannot forget a Plumbers Nightmare. Red Oak II was the brainchild of local artist Lowell Davis who actually grew up in the real Red Oak, Missouri. The original Red Oak, like many other rural towns, started to fade sometime after World War II.   In 1987, Davis's creative inspiration and empty cornfield farm led him to turn his acreage into a tribute to his boyhood hometown. He began to buy up the homes and businesses from the original town site and other rural ghost towns, moving them to the new site and with the help of others began restoring them to their original state. Davis has a love for the simpler times of the past that are reflected in the town as well as his paintings and sculptures. A couple of the buildings that are near and dear to Lowell's heart are the blacksmith shop, where his great-grandfather practiced his trade, and the General Store that was run by Lowell's father. Scattered about the town are several of Lowell's sculptures and old vehicles that appear frozen in time.   Davis still lives there in the Belle Starr house, where the infamous lady outlaw grew up.

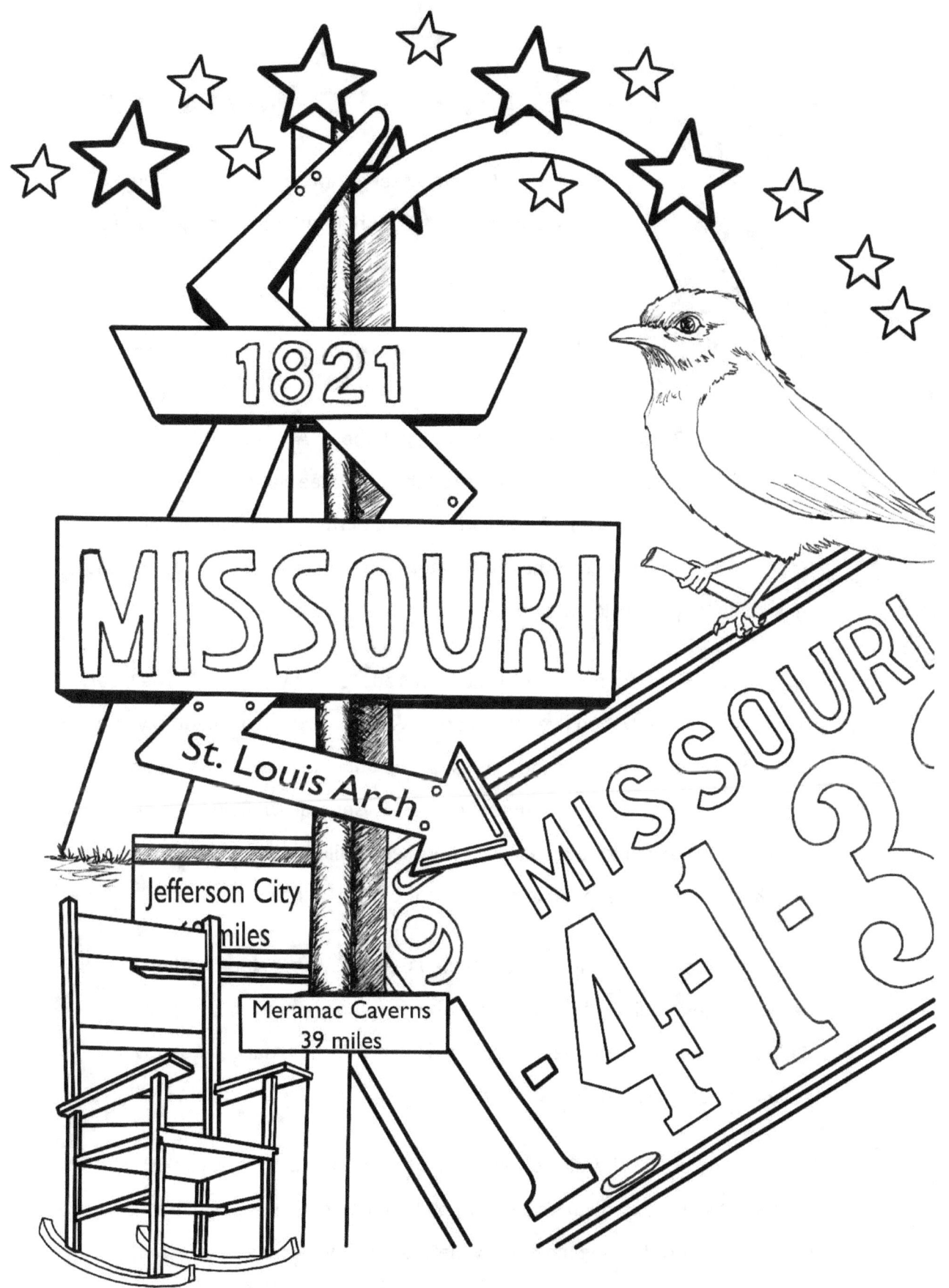

1821

MISSOURI

St. Louis Arch

Jefferson City

Meramac Caverns
39 miles

MISSOURI

Cherokee Nation

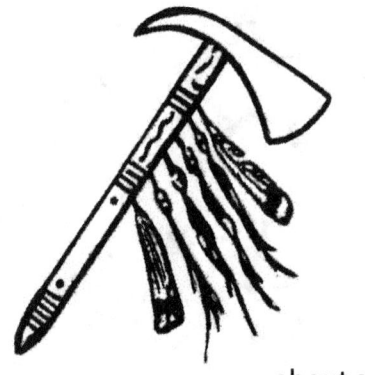

A sad chapter in American History. From Rolla to Springfield, Missouri, Route 66 wasn't just a road of dreams; it was a Trail of Tears. This is a story of racial

injustice, intolerance and suffering, but also a story about survival.

Passed by Congress, the Indian Removal Act of 1830 forever changed the Cherokee Nation. It provided the Cherokee Nation land west of the Mississippi river in exchange for what remained of their homeland in Eastern Georgia. The leaders of the Cherokee Nation fought against this act but by 1832 they knew they were defeated.

In 1836, the Treaty of New Echota was approved by congress. The treaty gave the Cherokee Nation five million dollars and two years to voluntarily move to the new relocation even though most of the Cherokee disagreed with the treaty and refused to move voluntarily. In 1838, General Winfield Scott and 7,000 soldiers began to round up the Cherokee families, uprooting them from their homes at bayonet point and carrying them off in chains.

Principal Chief John Ross petitioned General Scott to let the Cherokee people process their own removal. One by one, the Choctaw, Muscogee Creeks, Chickasaw and the Seminoles were forced from their homelands and moved to Indian Territory, now known as Oklahoma.

Over 16,000 Cherokees, divided into detachments of about 1,000 each, traveled 800 miles through nine states, by foot, horse, and wagon. The Cherokee suffered during the harsh winter and many died before reaching the new native lands.

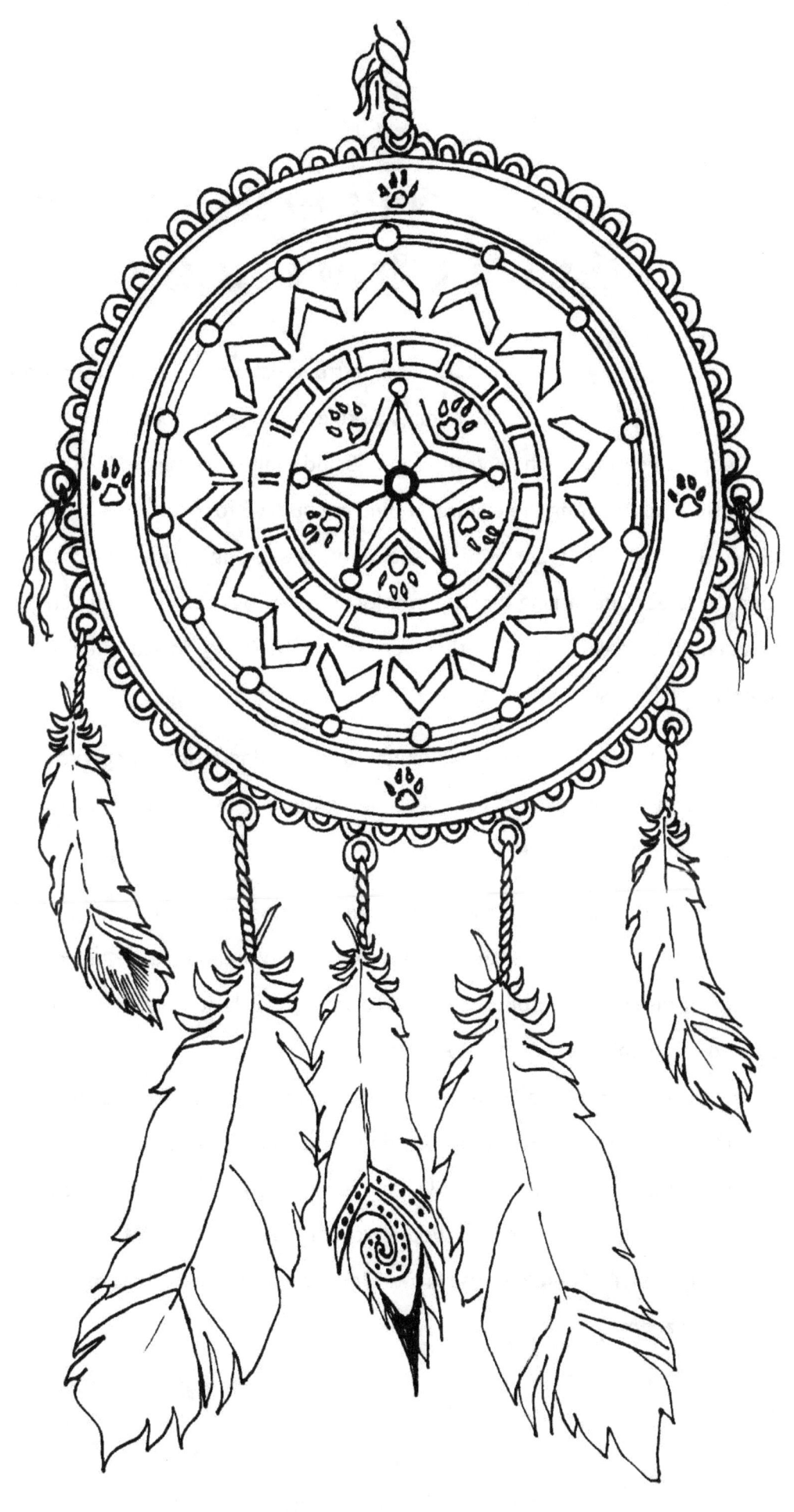

Legend of the Cherokee Rose

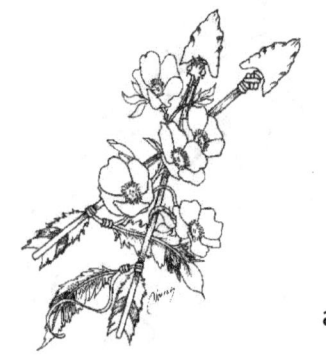

The trail to the West was long and treacherous and many were dying along the way. The Peoples' hearts were heavy with sadness and their tears mingled with the dust of the trail. Fearing the children would not survive to rebuild the Cherokee Nation without their mother's strength, the Elders called upon the Great One, asking for strength, for the grieving mothers of the Cherokee tribes and the weakling children that were sure to perish on this journey. The Elders asked for a sign of this strength.

The next day the woman watched as radiant blossoms formed, growing fast where the mother's tears had fallen. Covering the trail, the blossoms slowly Opened, vibrant and strong.

The five petal white blossom signified the tears that were shed, the golden center for the greed of the white man for the gold on their lands, seven green leaflets for the seven Cherokee clans, and a strong sturdy stem with stickers that would defy anything which tries to destroy it.

The mothers of the Cherokee forgot their sadness and like the plant they began to feel strong and beautiful. As the plant protected its blossoms with thorns, the mothers knew they would have the courage and determination to protect their children so that they would grow and begin a new Nation.
To this day the wild Cherokee rose grows along the route of the Trail of Tears into Eastern Oklahoma.

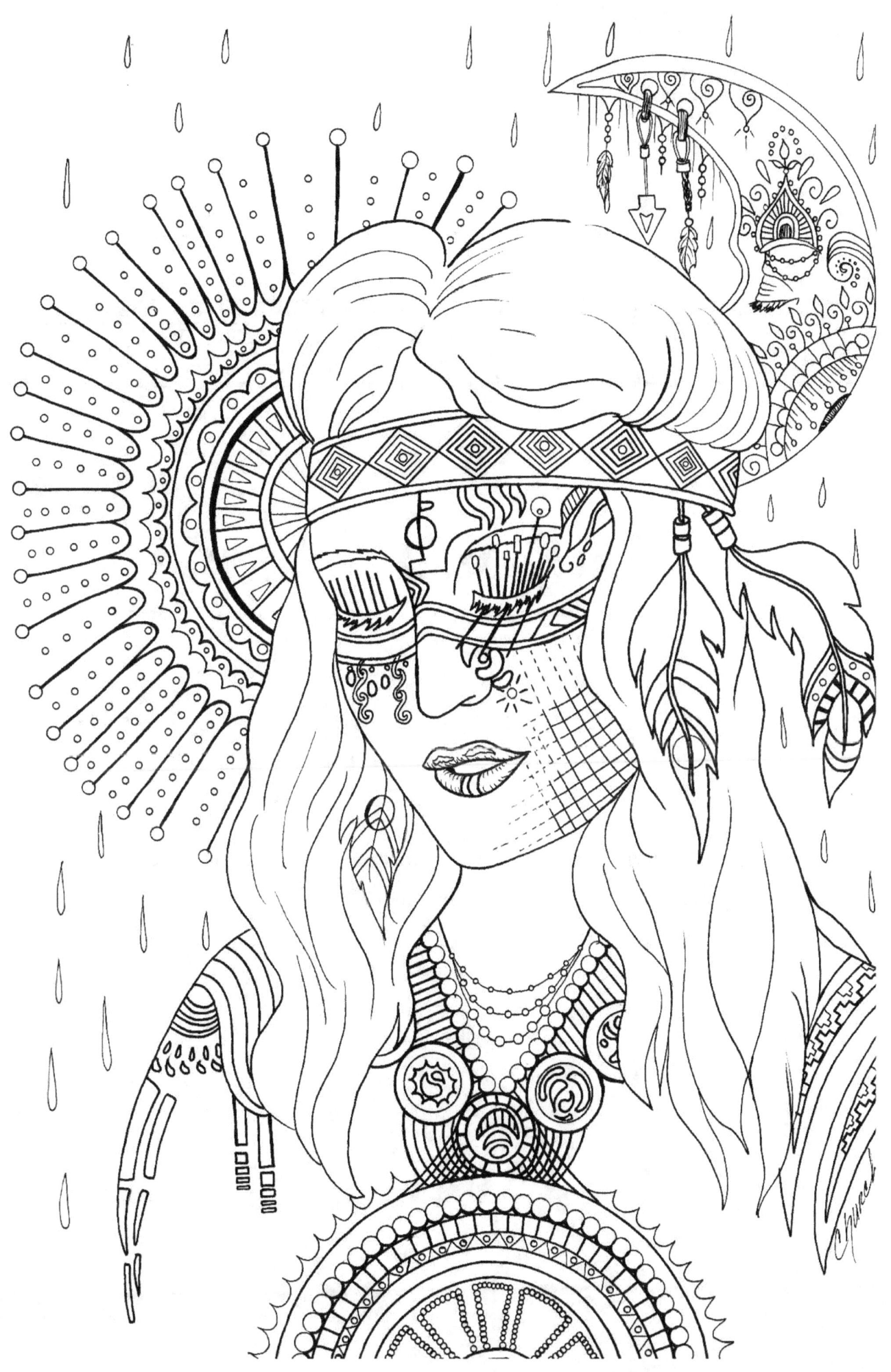

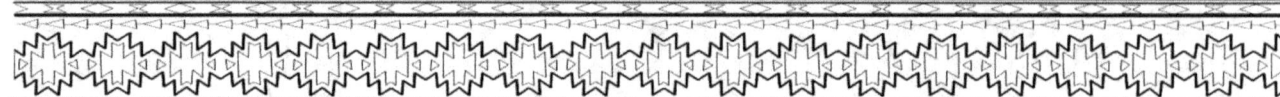

Tsalagihi Ayeli

The word Cherokee translates into "those who live in the mountains".

The Cherokee Nation is the largest tribe recognized in the United States, headquartered in Tahlequah, Oklahoma. The Nation has a tribal jurisdiction spanning over 14 counties in the northeastern corner of Oklahoma.

Today the Cherokee Nation has experienced an almost unprecedented expansion in economic growth and prosperity.

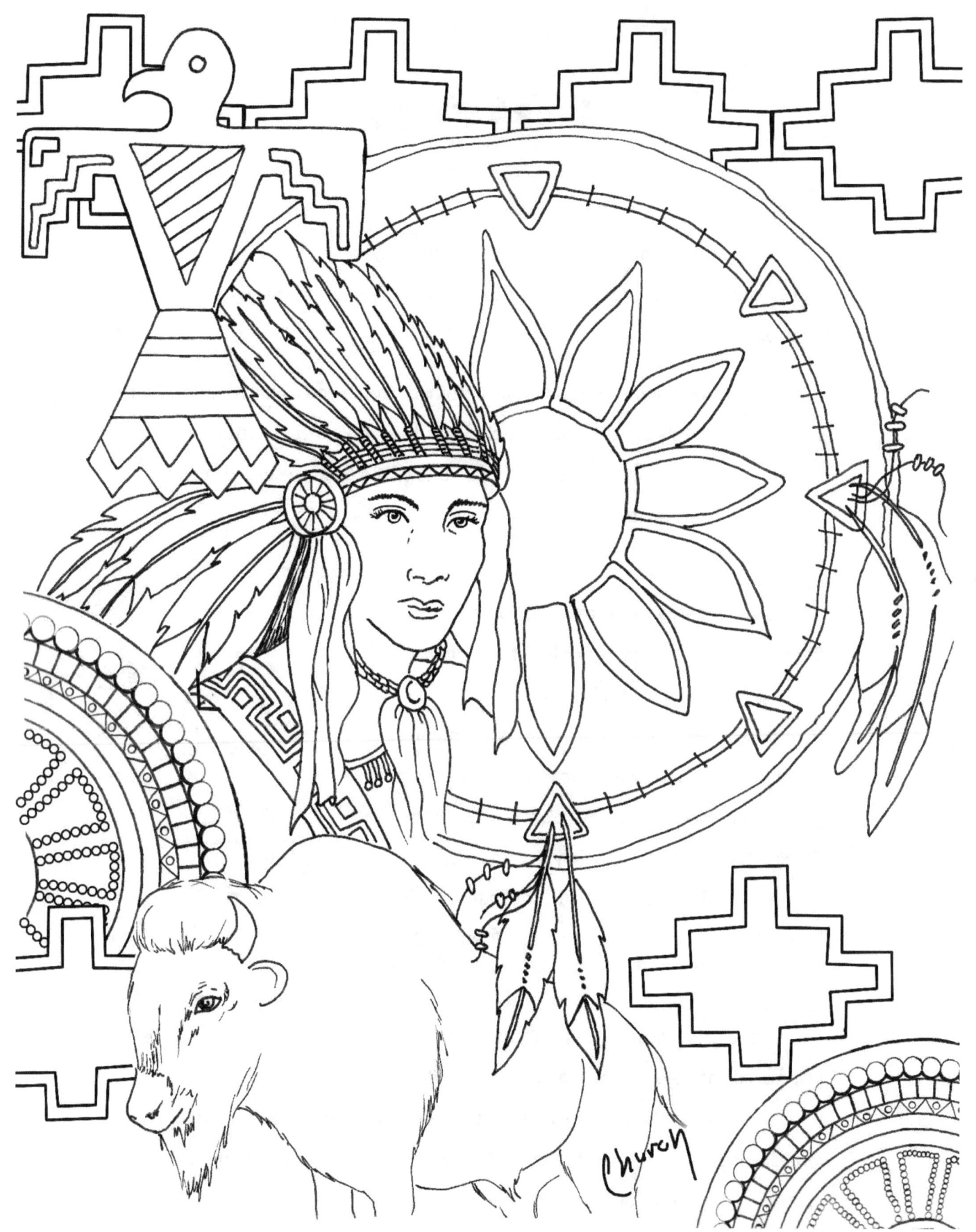

25

Kansas

"Ad Astra per Aspera" - "To the Stars through Difficulties"

The Sunflower State

Kansas became a state of the Union in 1861, being the 34th state to join. The Western Meadowlark, a familiar songbird of the open country, became the state bird in 1937.

Route 66 takes just a short thirteen-mile stretch across Kansas. The first state to completely pave the road by the year 1929, only 3 years after the development of the Route, it is to this day one of the best preserved sections of Route 66 and still holds a plethora of things to see.

Nestled at the foot of the Missouri Ozarks, the wooded area of Kansas was considered to be neutral lands for the Cherokee Indians. It was quickly settled when a mineral containing lead sulfide, also known as Galena, was discovered in the area. With mining in full swing a small town developed. As the town grew, the named changed to "*Cornwall*", "*Short Creek*", "*Bonanza*", followed by the final name, "*Galena*". The track of road to the oldest mining town of Kansas used to be known as "Hell's Half Acre".

The Eagle Picher Smelter Plant and the 215 feet long, 1923 viaduct all sit just outside of Galena. The lead mining and Route 66 brought prosperity and a population of about 30,000 people. After the Great Depression, exhausted mines, and the I-44 bypass, the flow of travelers slowed down. The once thriving community's population dropped to meager 3,000, almost a ghost town.

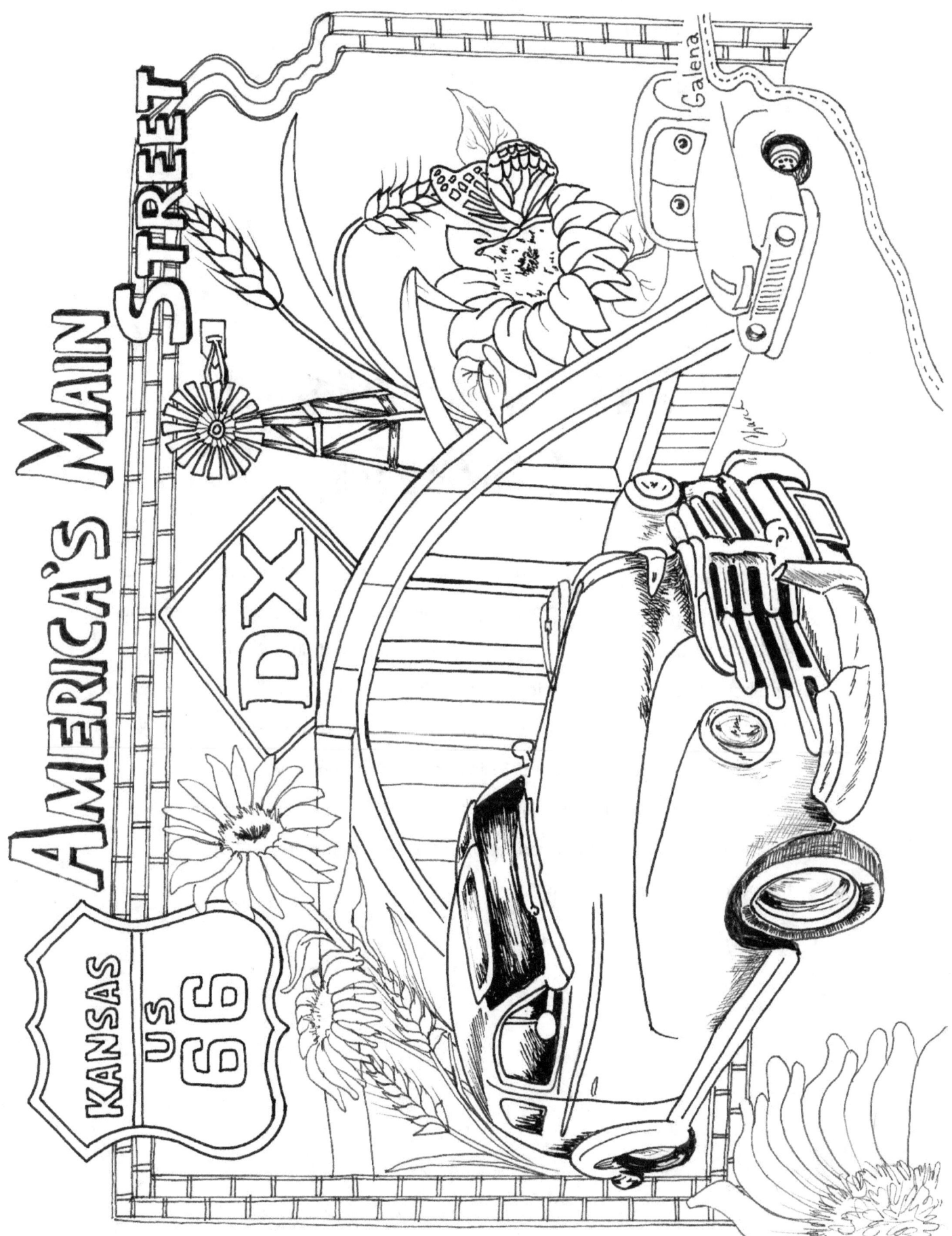

The Streets of Galena

Today there are still several of the original buildings standing; while many remain abandoned, some are now repurposed. Just as you enter the town, there are three interesting old buildings at the intersection of Route 66 and Main Street. One being the Kan-O-Tex service station, which is on the south side of the town. Restored and renamed *Cars on the Route*, it now offers souvenirs and a snack bar. Outside of the facility is a 1951 International Boom Truck, which inspired the "Tow Mater" character in the Disney movie Cars. The Kan-O-Tex service station sits in front of an abandoned warehouse that served as a hideaway for the outlaws Bonnie and Clyde.

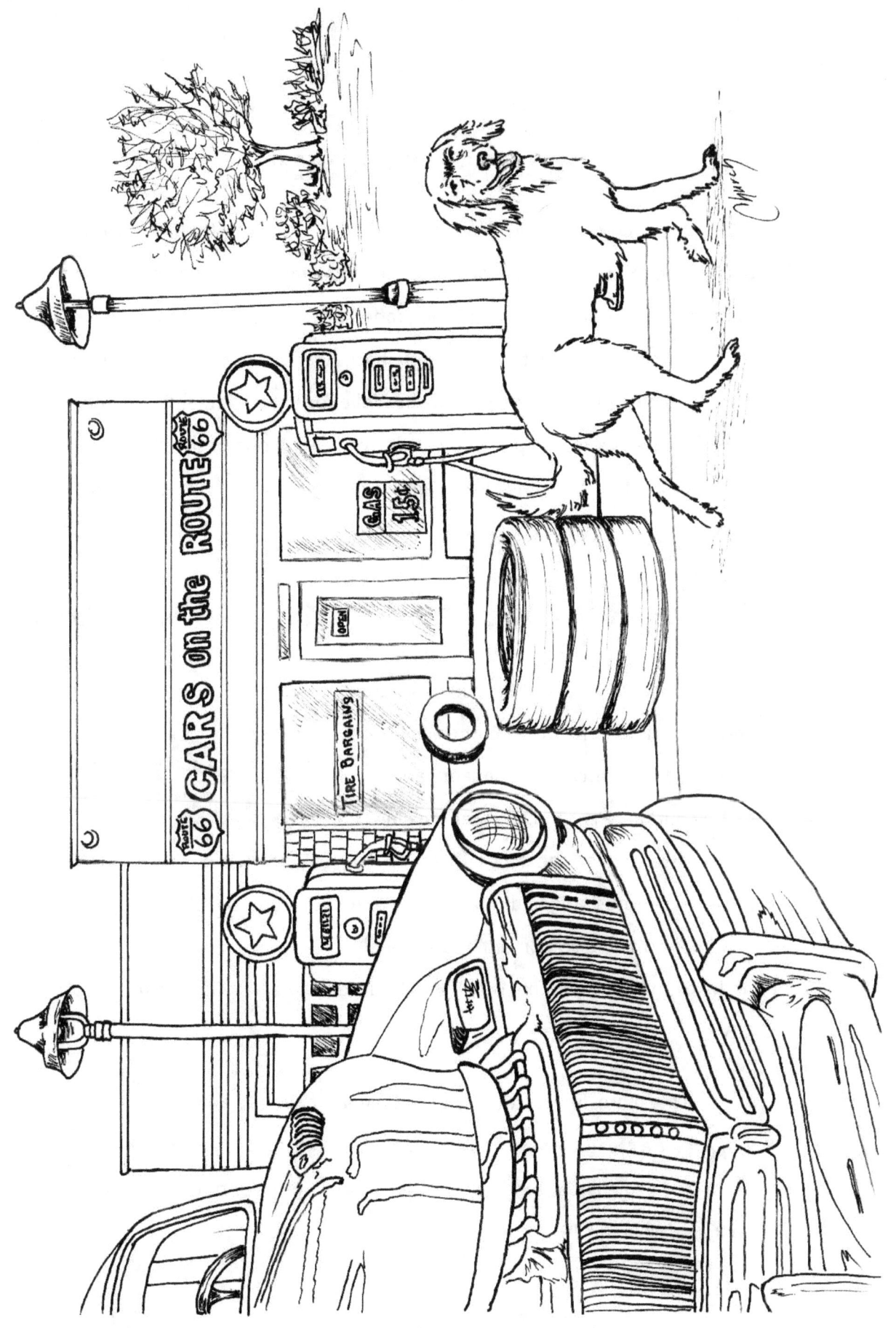

Murder Bordello

According to legend, Galena's bordello was built in 1890 and was run by a family of murderers. The bordello was built by a mining company and was said to have been a workman's perk. The Staffelback family was hired by the mining company to run the facility.   The Staffelbacks were said to have murdered more than 30 miners that had come to the bordello for entertainment. The murdered miner's bodies were dumped in the area mines, with one of the mines located on the property. The family was eventually caught and went to prison, but only for the murder of one man.

The Galena Mining & Historical Museum

Occupying an old Missouri-Texas-Kansas railroad depot relocated from another location on Route 66, the Galena Mining and Historical Museum appears to be tiny but there is a much larger building tucked away behind the depot. The museum features unique displays of mineral specimens, mining equipment and a model of the Grand Central Mine, which was located just east of Galena in Central City.

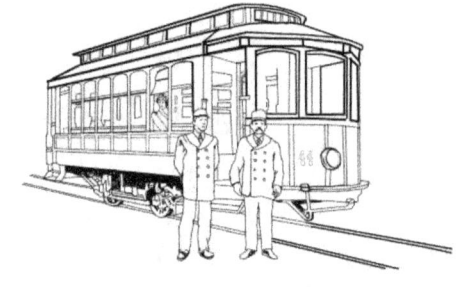

One more "must stop" while in Galena, for coffee lovers or those just looking for a great, chic atmosphere to relax, Streetcar Station might be the right place. The name is derived from the streetcars that used to run through Galena on Route 66 in the 1920's and 30's.

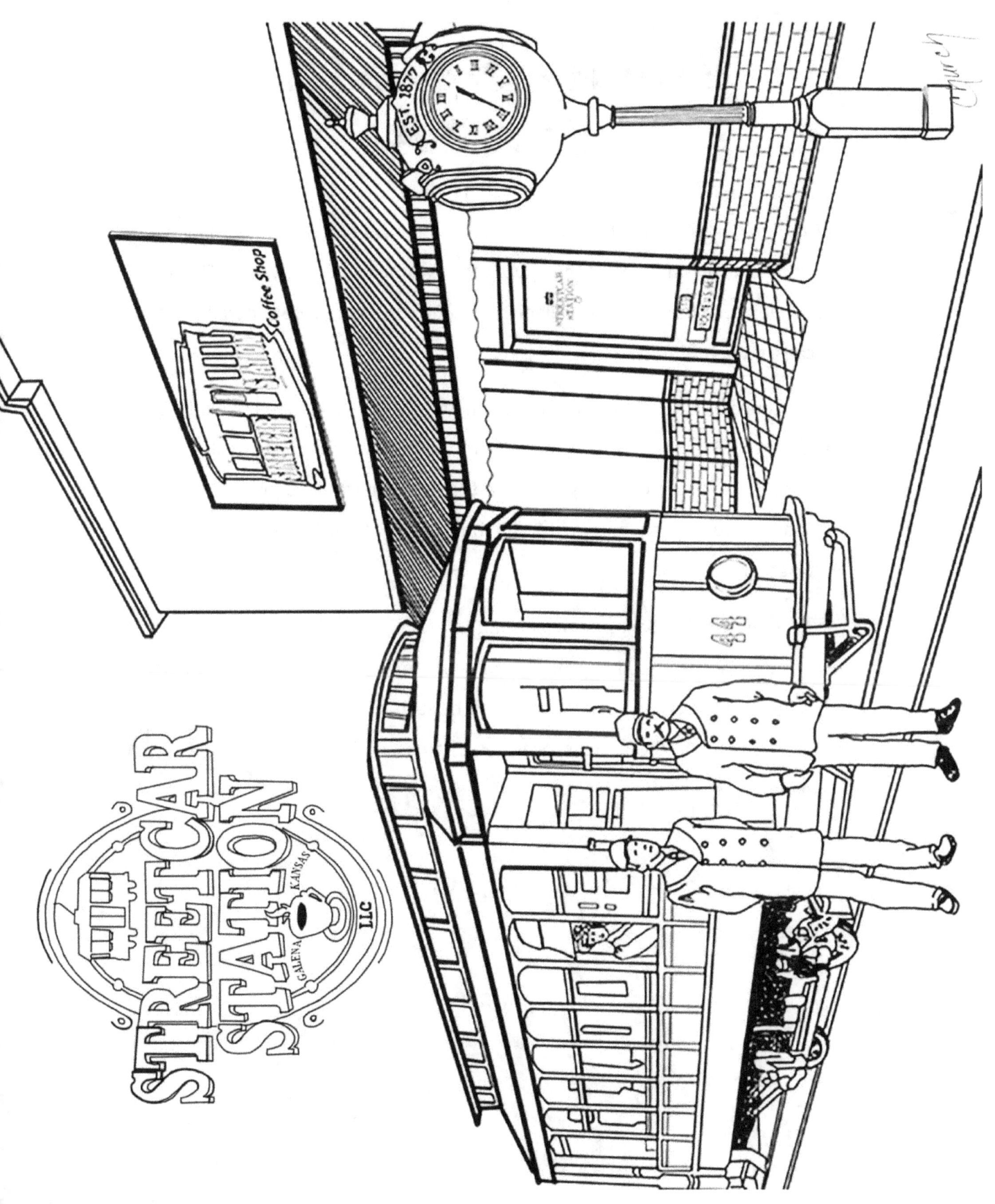

31

Riverton & Baxter Springs

Eisler Brother's Old Riverton Store in Riverton, Kansas has been operating along Historic Route 66 since before the Route officially opened. Built by Leo Williams in 1925, operating the market as Williams Store until 1973 when Joe and Isabell Eisler purchased the business.

One of the most exquisite sites along the route in Kansas is a one of a kind Marsh Arch Bridge, built in 1923, also known as the Rainbow Bridge near Riverton. Even though the bridge is closed to the main traffic today, you can still drive across due to its rescue in 1992 by the Kansas Historic Route 66 Association.

In downtown Baxter Springs along Route 66, you will find small plaques explaining the history of the buildings, which include banks and businesses robbed by such infamous robbers as Bonny & Clyde, Henry Star, Jesse James, and Cole Younger.

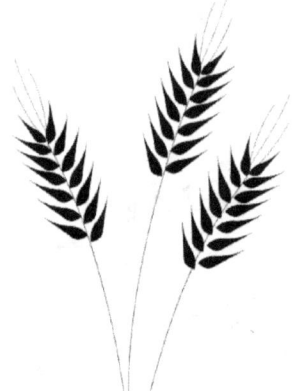

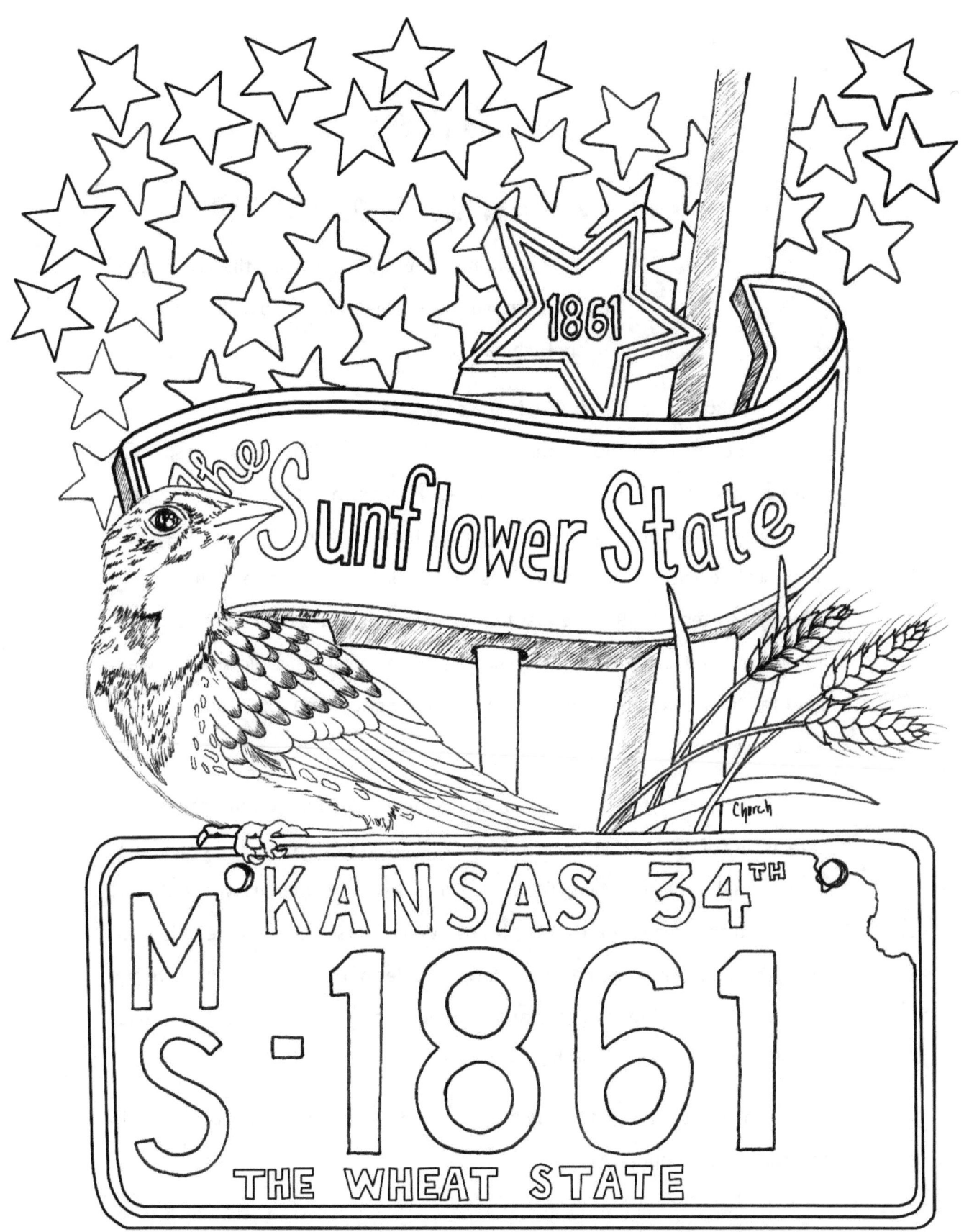

Route 66 & Will Rogers Highway

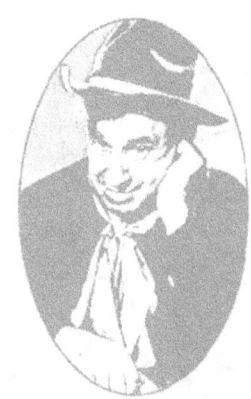

A portion of Route 66 runs along the Will Rogers Turnpike but was once itself referred to as the Will Rogers Highway.

Will Rogers, known as Oklahoma's favorite son, was born into a prominent Cherokee Nation family in Indian Territory of Oklahoma. He spent his youth in and around Route 66 communities. He was one of the most widely read newspaper writers of his time, offering dry, whimsical commentaries on a variety of political, social, and economic issues, and he became the voice of the "average" citizen. By 1933, he was the top male box-office draw in the United States movie industry. After Will died in a 1935 plane crash, radio stations went silent for 30 minutes out of respect for one of America's most quoted broadcasters.

Prior to Rogers's death, Oklahoma leaders asked him to represent the state as one of their two statues in the Capitol. Rogers's agreed, but only if the image would be placed facing the House Chamber. His comment was so that he could keep an eye on congress. To this day Will Rogers's statue is the only statue facing the Chamber entrance. According to guides of the Capitol, each governor rubs the left shoe of the Rogers statue for good luck before entering the House Chamber to give the State of the State address.

The most used quote by Will Rogers: "I don't make jokes. I just watch the government and report the facts."

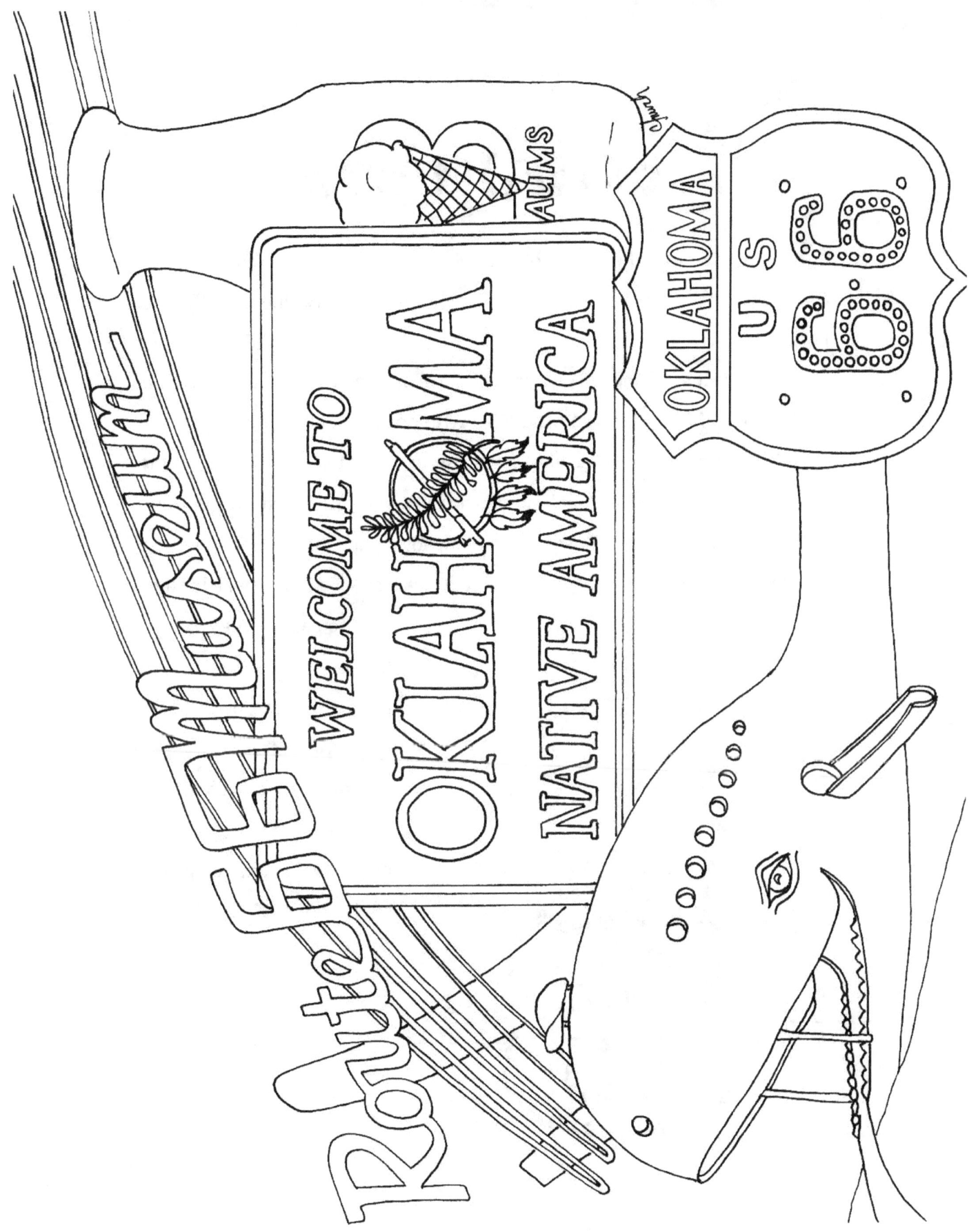

35

Oklahoma

Route 66 runs the stretch of 400 miles across the state of Oklahoma. Oklahoma obtained its name from two Choctaw Indian words meaning "Red People."

The Father of Route 66 was said to have been an Oklahoma businessman by the name of Cyrus Avery (1871-1963). Cyrus and his family journeyed west from Pennsylvania by covered wagon to Missouri and later settled in Oklahoma. He made a living in farming, real estate, and oil, among other ventures. Cyrus was a big part of the Good Roads Movement, advocating for the highway, developing a national system of numbered highways as well as pushing for the

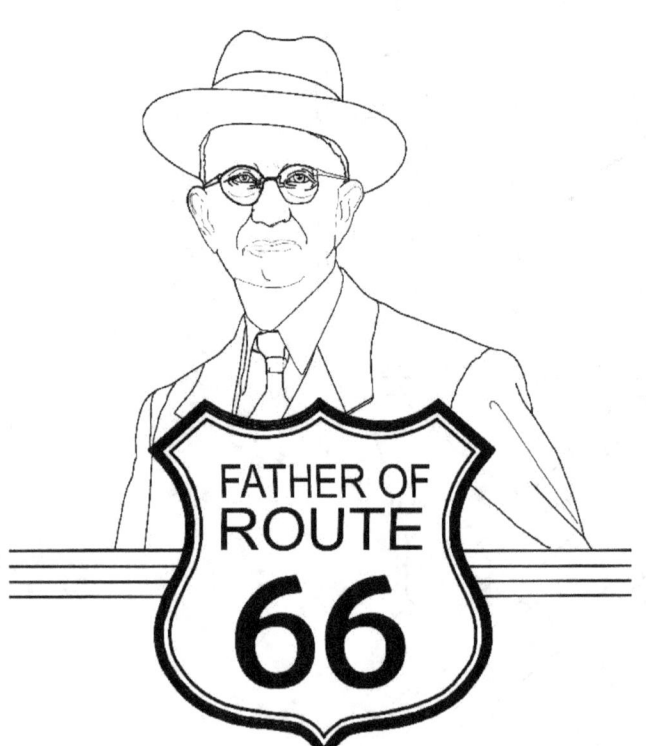

road to pass through Oklahoma. To boost tourism on the roadway, he titled the road "Main Street of America." Cyrus also pushed to get the entire highway paved, which was completed by the late 1930's.

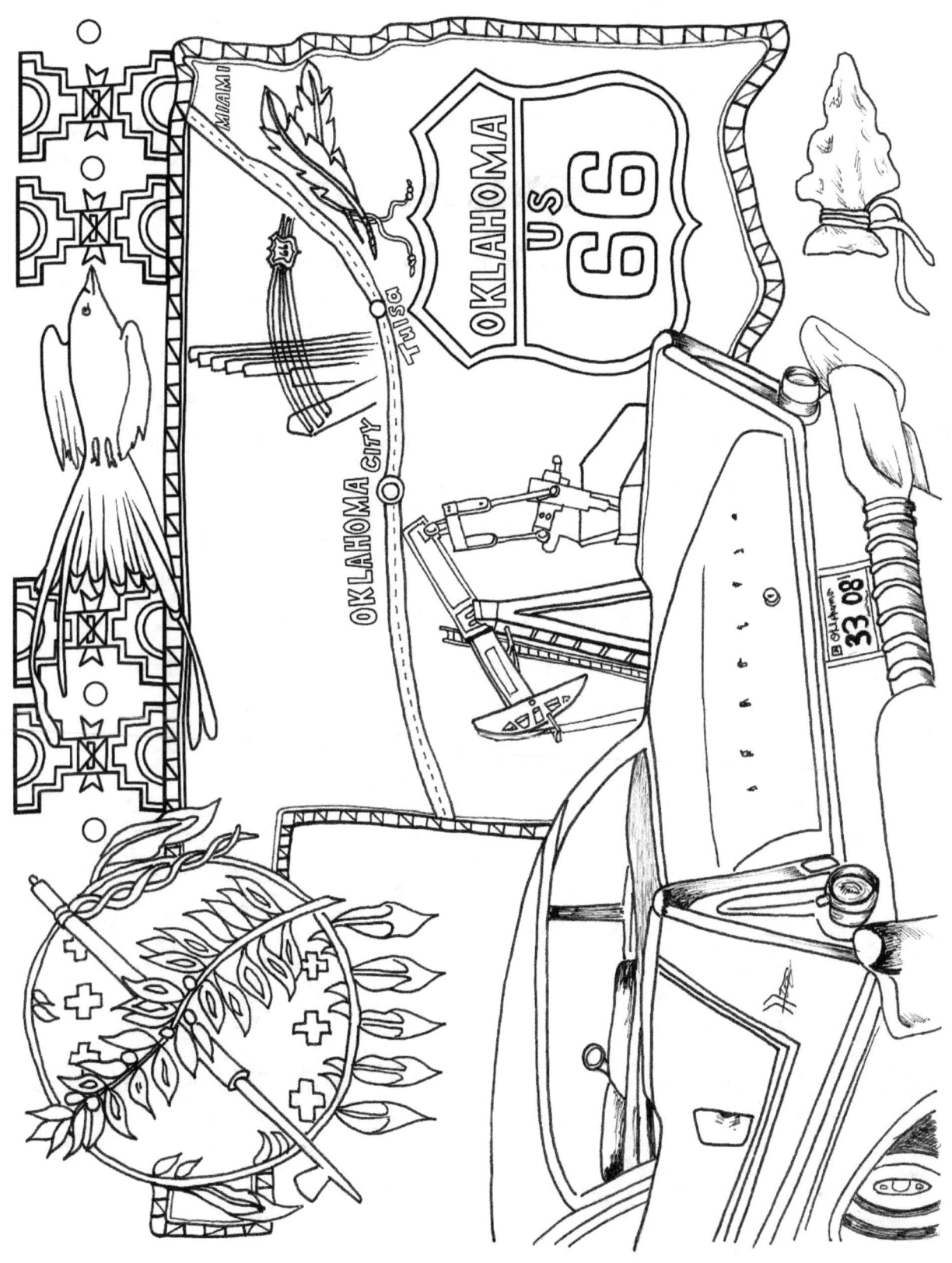

Oklahoma

State flower – mistletoe

The land of Oklahoma, where the state animals, the scissor-tailed flycatcher and the bison, roam. Throughout the 19th century, the U.S. government relocated Indian tribes to the area and by 1900 over 30 Indian tribes called home to what originally known as the Indian Territories. Ranchers from Texas were in search of more pasture lands leading to the government opening up the land for settlement, creating "land runs" in which settlers were allowed to cross the border at a particular hour to claim homesteads. Settlers who broke the law and crossed the border sooner than allowed were referred to as "sooners," which eventually became the state's nickname.

Oklahoma became the 46th state in 1907. The state flag illustrates the rich Native American culture.

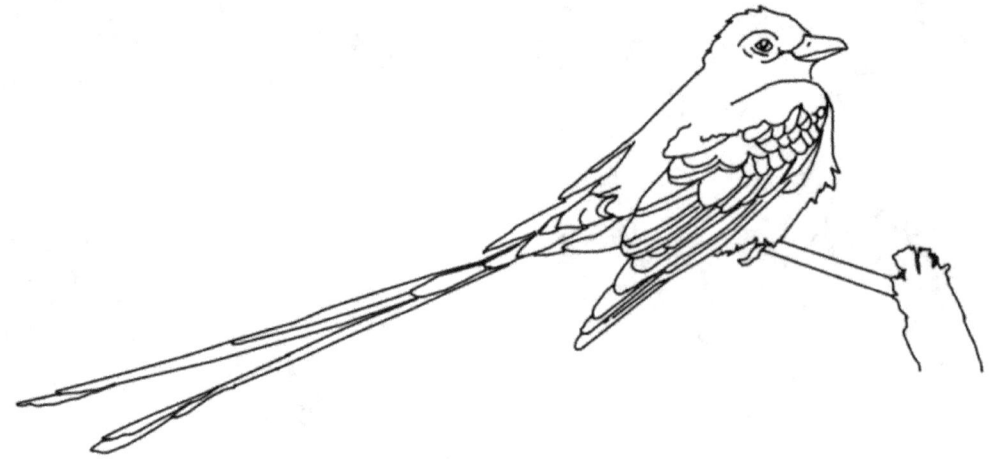

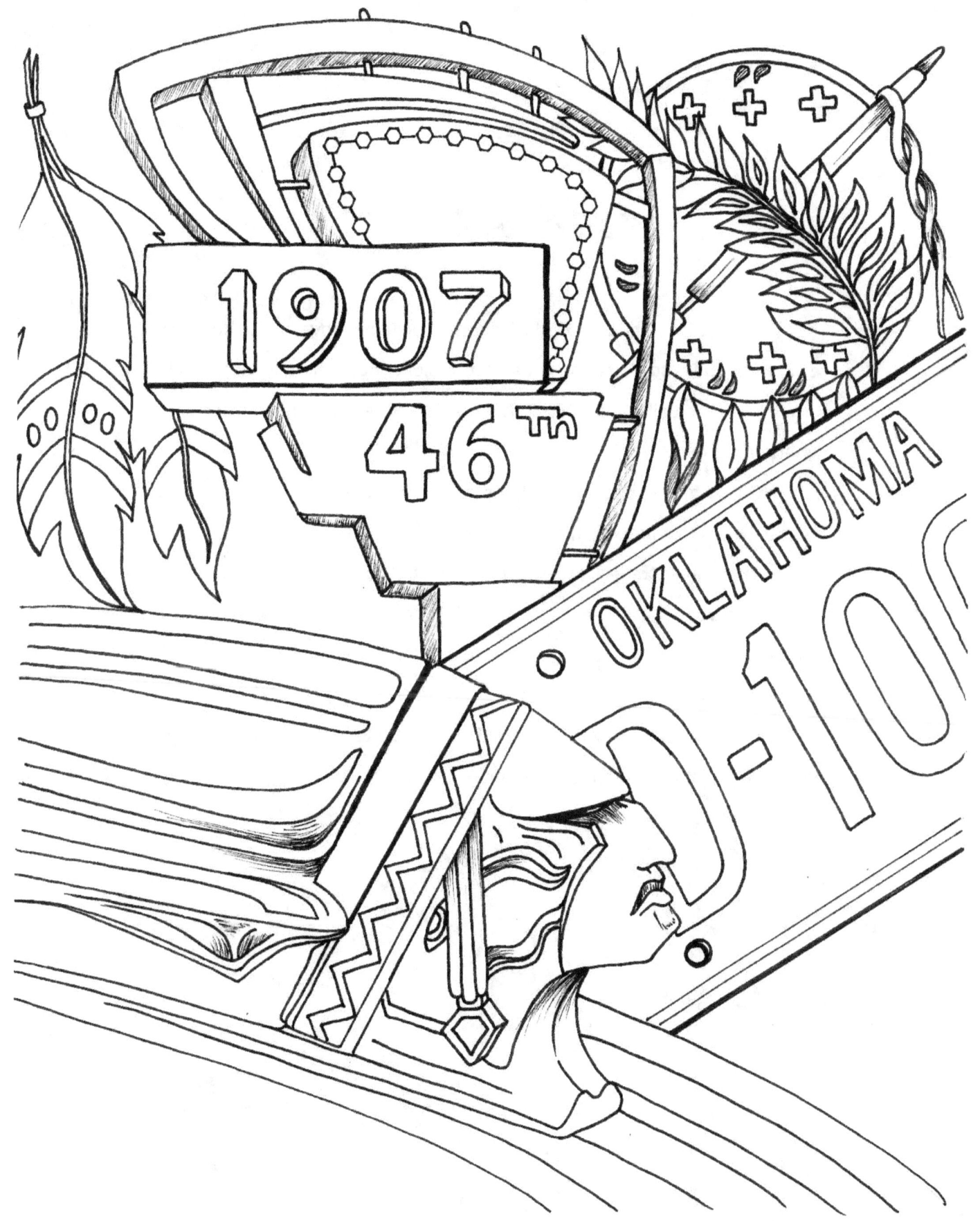

"Black Gold"

In the 1930s, thousands of Oklahoma residents moved to California as a result of the Dust Bowl and the Great Depression. They were known as "Okies," a term that was initially derogatory but became a badge of pride for later generations.

Oil has always been one of the main commodities of Oklahoma. For the longest time Oklahoma was the largest oil producer in the country.

Oklahoma's state capitol building is the only capitol with an oil well directly underneath it. In 1941, the "Petunia Number One" well was slant drilled through a flowerbed to reach the oil pool, which produced approximately 1.5 million bbl. over the course of 43 years.

It is only fitting that there should be a page honoring the fuel industry and the years of fuel pump changes and shapes.

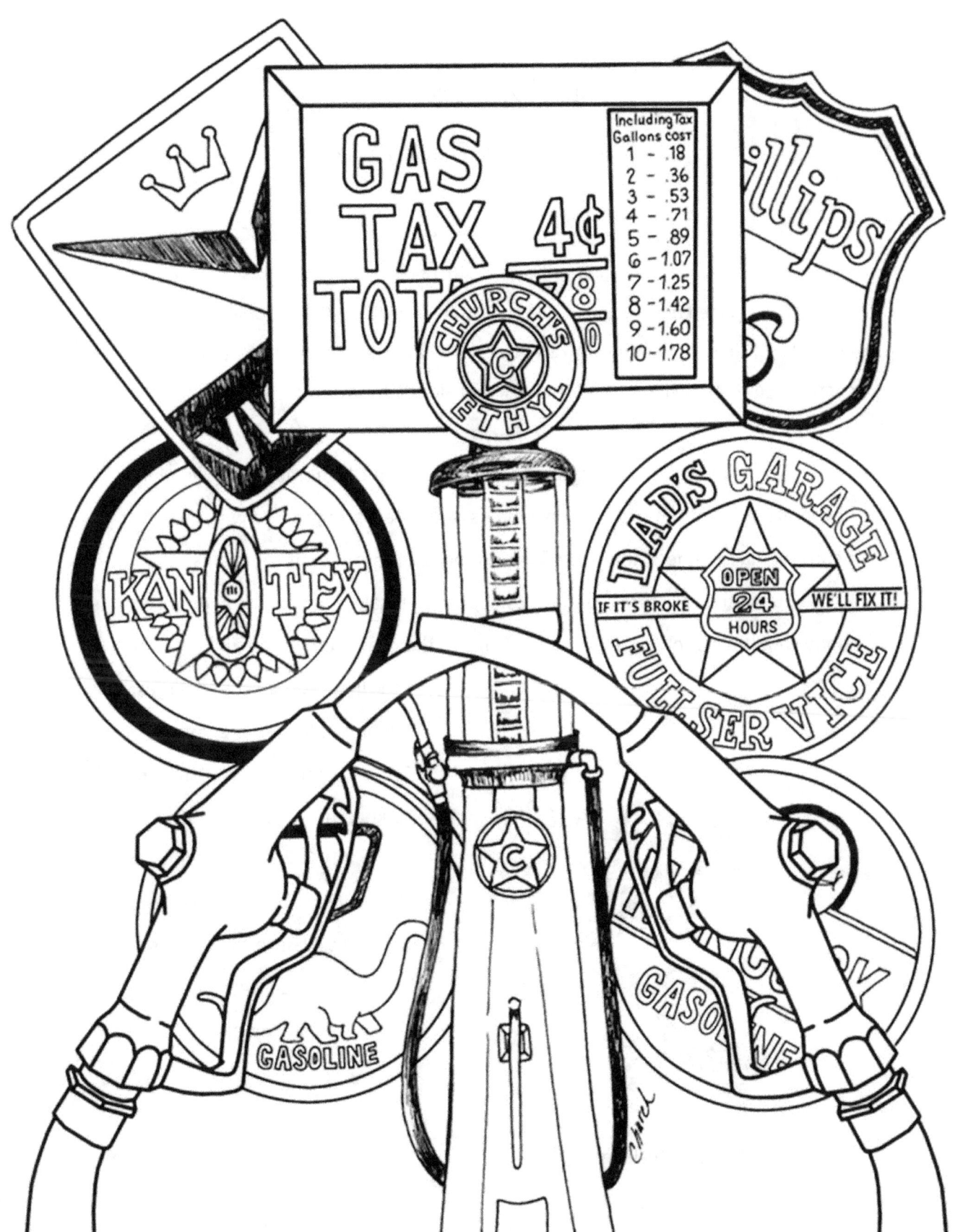

Texas

Dum spiro spero ("While I breathe, I hope")

Texas became part of the United States on December 29, 1845, an event which sparked the Mexican-American War (1846-1848).

Texas gained the nickname "The Lone Star" from its brief years of independence (1836-1845). In fact, according to Texas history, at one point Texas territory had been controlled by three different nations: France, Spain and Mexico.

You know when you have entered Texas from Oklahoma; the rolling hills have flattened out entering the vast plains of the Texas Panhandle with the beautiful Blue Bonnets, the state flower, blooming throughout the plains. Old Route 66 stretched across the Llano Estacado (the staked plains) through the many small cattle towns. In relation of size to the other states, the 28th state of the Union is the second largest, encompassing an area of 268,581 square miles. In order to keep from getting lost on the Panhandle's 200-mile stretch of flat plains, early travelers would drive a stake into the earth to mark their route, giving it the nickname "staked plains."

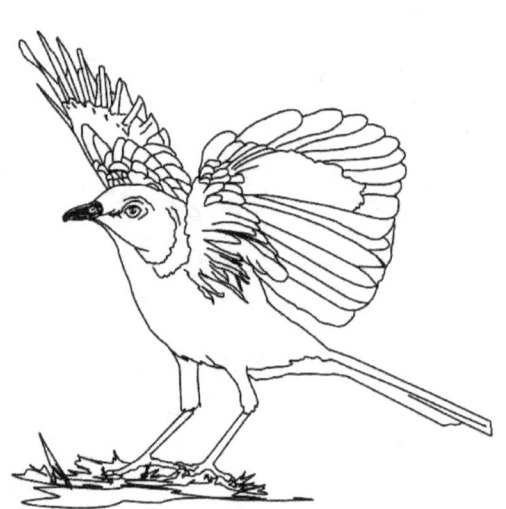

State Bird ~ Mockingbird

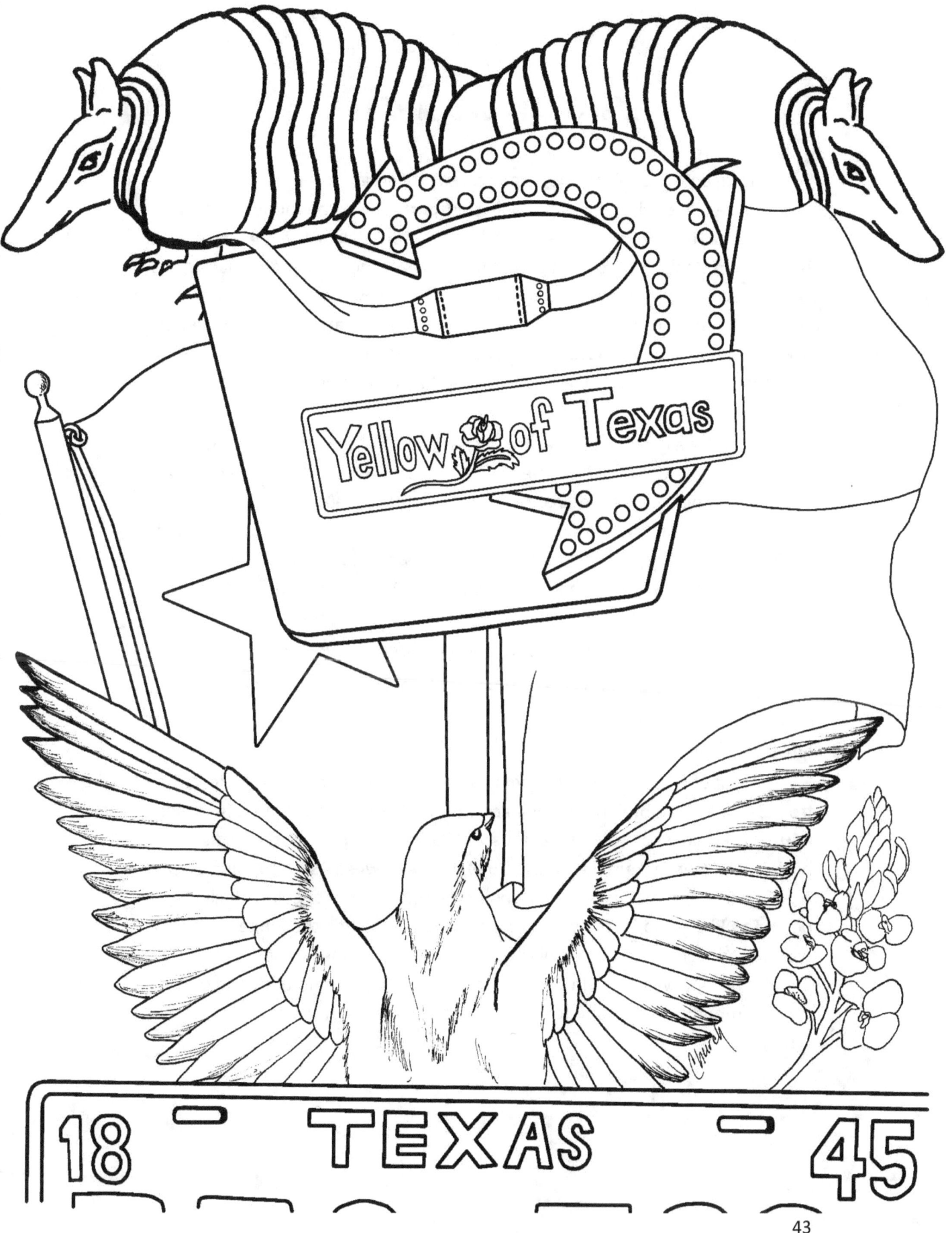

Yellow of Texas

18 - TEXAS - 45

43

The Panhandle

Long before brick pavers, asphalt, reflective signs, mile markers and passing lanes, the railroad was the only transportation throughout Texas. The first train rails hit the Panhandle ground in the 1880's. In 1902, the Pacific Railroad laid tracks east to west across the plains of the Panhandle, placing the roadbed and rails on top of nine county lines. Route 66 more or less followed the rails. It became the evacuation route for the displaced farmers during the Dust Bowl days of the Great Depression. When I-40 was built it drained the life-force from the smaller towns and businesses, resulting in abandoned towns, ruins and, ghosts.

The Texas Panhandle was the farthest southern extent of the buffalo rich grasslands of the Great Plains. The Kiowa and Comanche Indians called this area home. Today oil and gas production, as well as trucking and Route 66 tourism, have joined ranching as the region's economic base. From the Oklahoma line to the New Mexico line, the 178 miles of Route 66 was traveled by many, from desperados to folks seeking a new life. Surprisingly enough, today 90% of the original highway remains.

Once you hit Adrian, Texas from either direction, you are at mid-point. McLean, Texas, home of the Texas Route 66 Association, houses the Devil's Rope Museum/ Texas Route 66 Exhibit complex, the old Avalon Theater, and the first Phillips 66 station.

West of Amarillo you will find an art installation from 1974. Three artists from San Francisco buried ten Cadillacs nose first into a Texas wheat field along I-40. With each version of the famous Cadillac tail fin up in air, the Cadillacs are buried in sequence from the oldest, 1949, to the newest, 1964, totaling 10 cars. The Cadillacs have been painted several times in a variety of colors, including pink. The Pink period was by far the most popular, lasting the longest before it was tagged. Because of high growth in Amarillo, the property that held the Caddies became valuable. In 1977 the property was sold and the Caddies were moved from the original site to a new spot two miles west but still along the interstate.

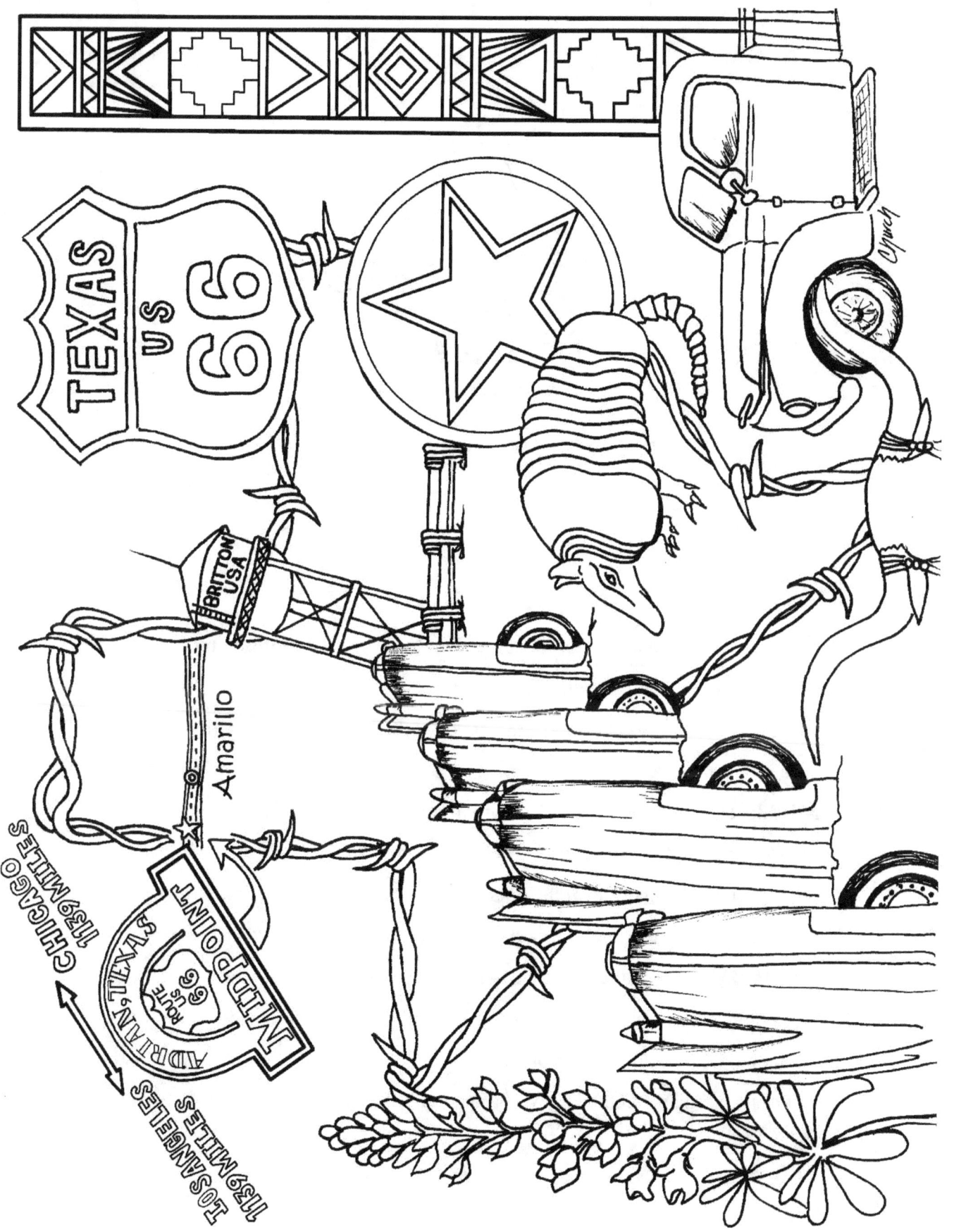

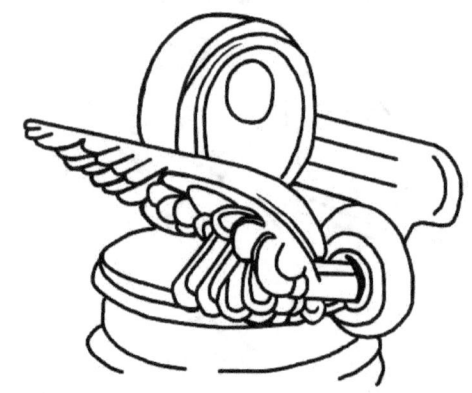

Hood Bonnet

The first "hood ornament" was a sun-crested falcon (to bring good luck) mounted on King Tut's chariot.

In the beginning, automobiles had moto-meters. A moto-meter was a thermometer that screwed into the radiator cap and was quite ugly. The purpose of the moto-meter was to inform the driver of the engine's temperature. Automobile makers began sprucing them up over time, adding wings, knobs, and other decorations. By the 1920's, moto meters were no longer necessary; the gage was moved to the dashboard of the automobile. The caps for the radiators were still on the top of the grille, outside of the hood, making it essential to utilize the design element to hide the radiator cap, personalizing the vehicle in the process. By the 50's auto makers began moving towards the smoother, chic look. Consequently the ornaments became a more abstract, spear-like decoration such as Chief Indian heads, rockets, or winged women. The 1958 Chevy Bel-Air was the first car released off of the line with the hood ornament missing. It was a sign of change.

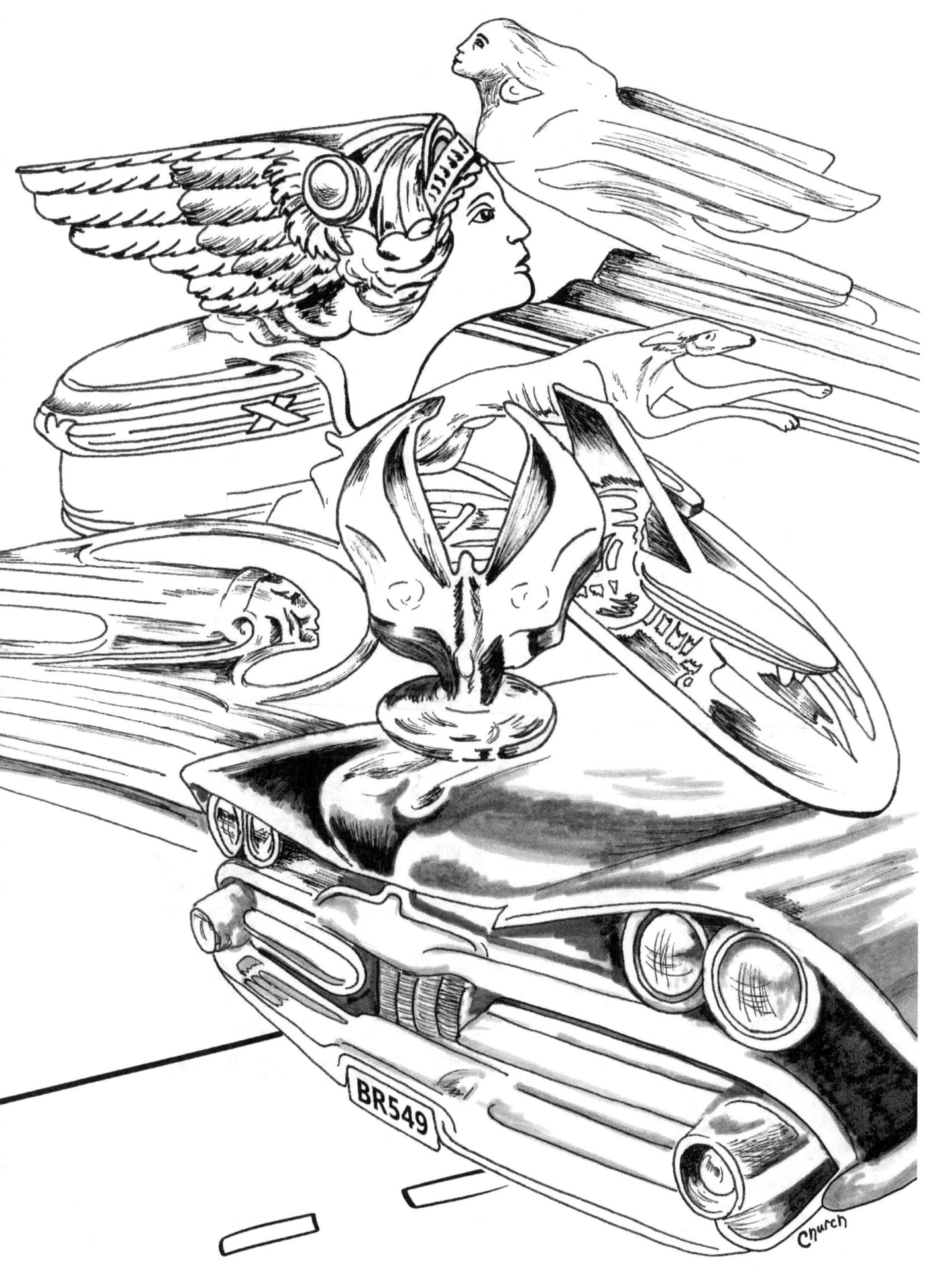

New Mexico

Motto Credscit eundo (It grows as it goes)

State flower – yucca

With a wide variety of landscapes: the breathtaking mountain ranges, sandstone mesas, desert sagebrush, ponderosa pines, and ghost towns, the New Mexico Route 66 is definitely one to remember.

New Mexico was admitted into the Union as the 47th State in 1912, with a rich history of ancient and contemporary cultures. Traditions ranging from Indian, Spanish and Mexican, New Mexico is an important center of Indian culture. The main groups are Navajo, Apache and Pueblo. Route 66 was the life blood to the communities, providing resources and materials. This two lane black top was the backbone of the economic development of the hundreds of communities along the Route which tracked along portions of the Trail of the Ancient Byways. In the beginning, the Route originally went through Santa Fe, the capital of New Mexico, until 1937. This original section was 506 miles and was mostly unpaved road. Albuquerque began pushing for a straighter route. In 1931, federal money was allocated to realign the road with a more east and west direction right through Albuquerque, dropping the miles down to 465.

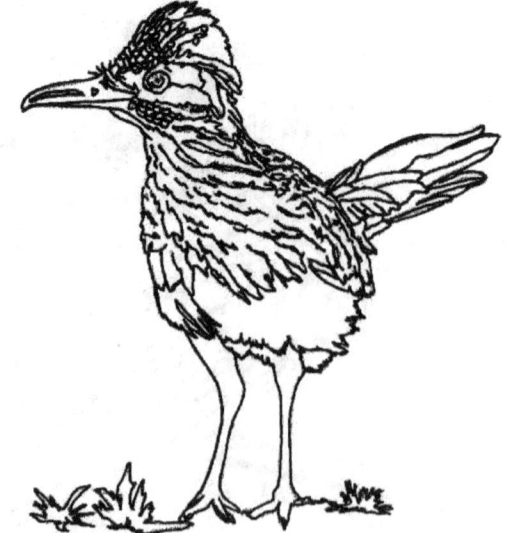

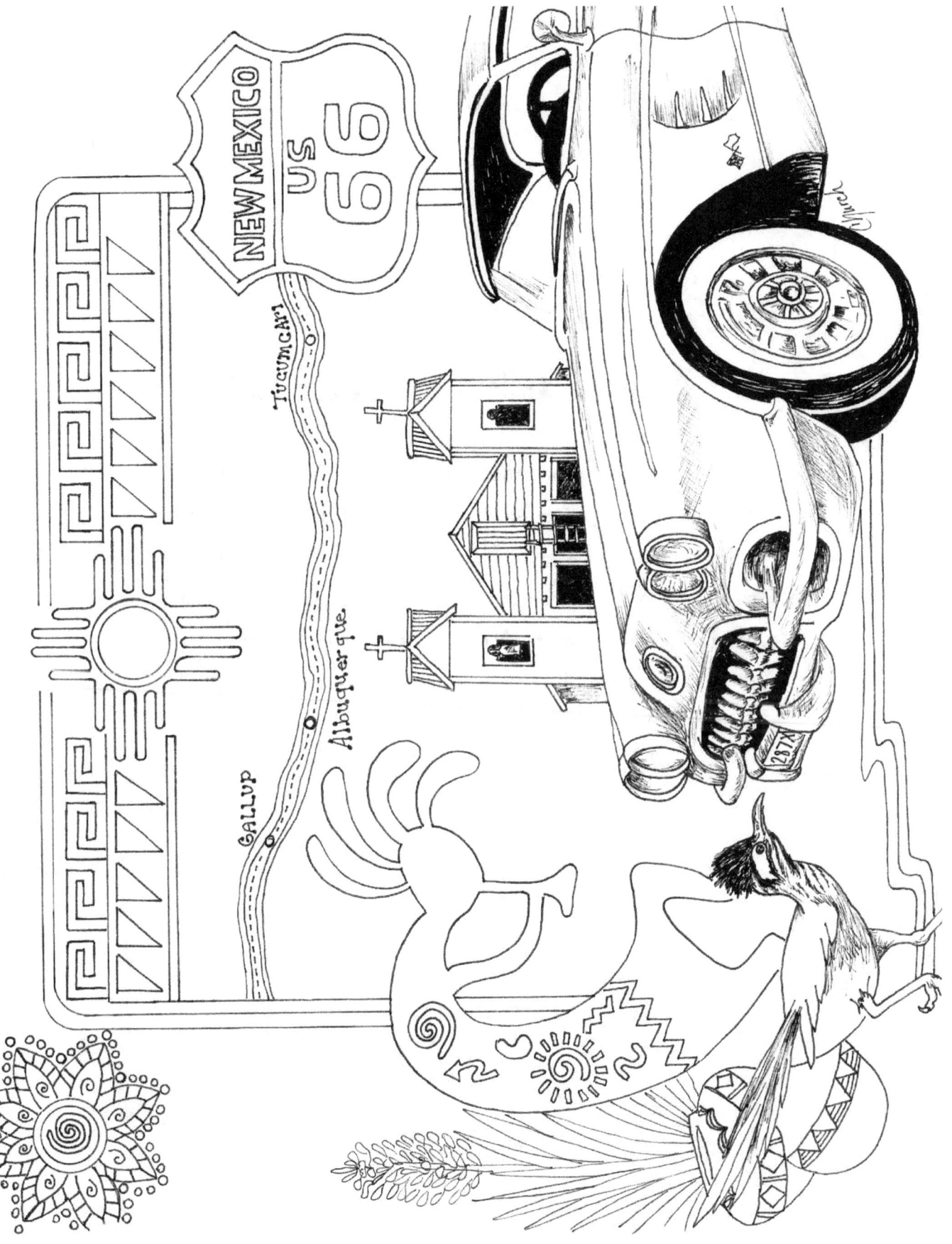

49

The Oldest Church

Built in 1610, the San Miguel Mission in Santa Fe is the oldest church in the United States. The church, constructed under the supervision of Franciscan friars, initially serv a small congregation of soldiers, laborers, and Indians who lived in the Analco Barrio. The adobe church was partially destroed during the Pueblo Revolt of 1680. It was rebuilt and restored in 1710 and has gone through many restorations over the past 400 years.

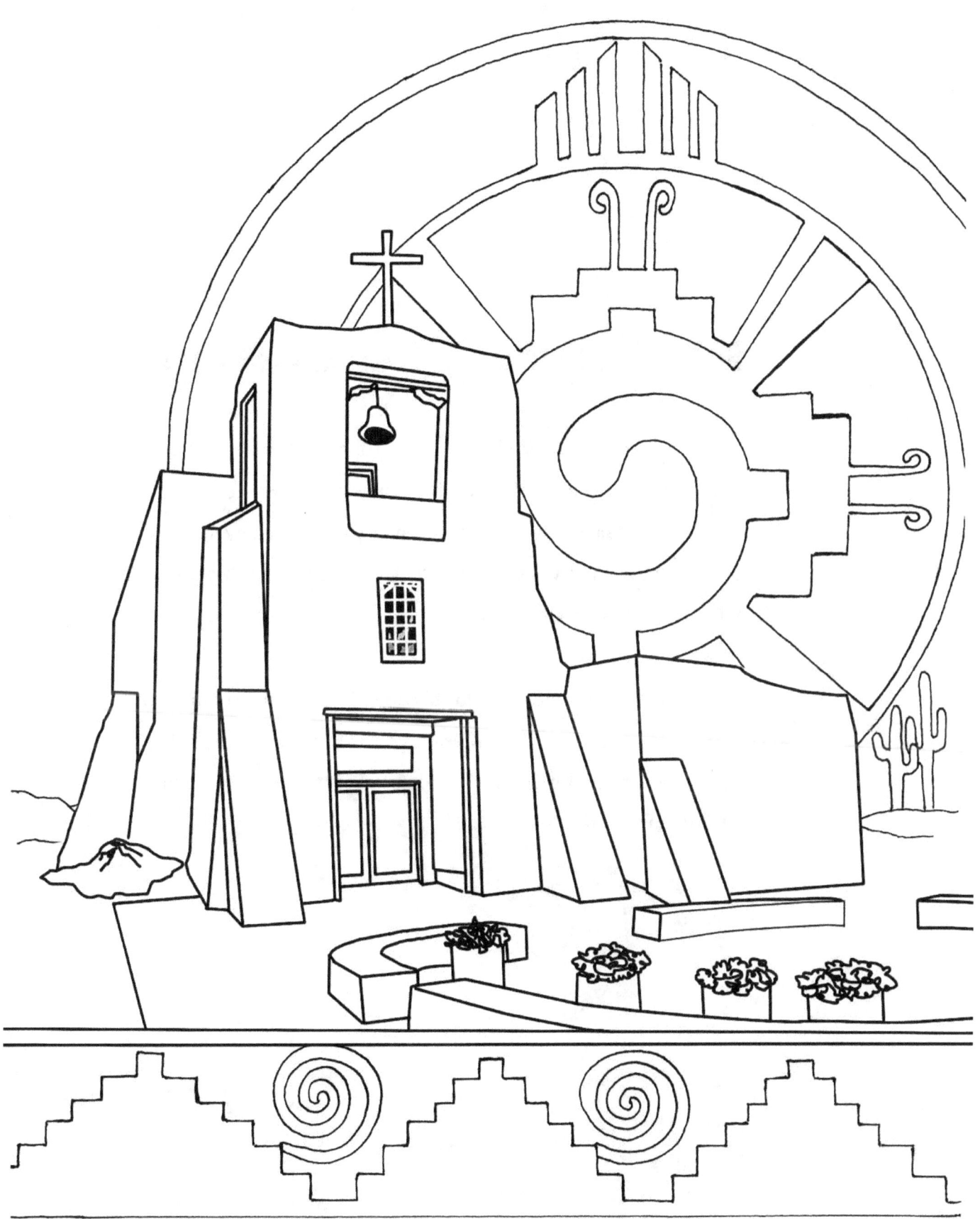

The Land of Enchantment

New Mexico is a beautiful state with all of the colors and terrains. Some interesting facts about the New Mexico portion of Route 66 is that some of the mountain passes became legendary and feared by motorists, who often found themselves stranded. New Mexico is the only state where Route 66 crosses itself at Central Avenue and Fourth street downtown Albuquerque.

It is rare that a business would stay open 90 years and running but on First Street in Tucumcari, New Mexico, you will find a Texaco station that is the only service station to have operated continuously through the Route 66 era to the present day.

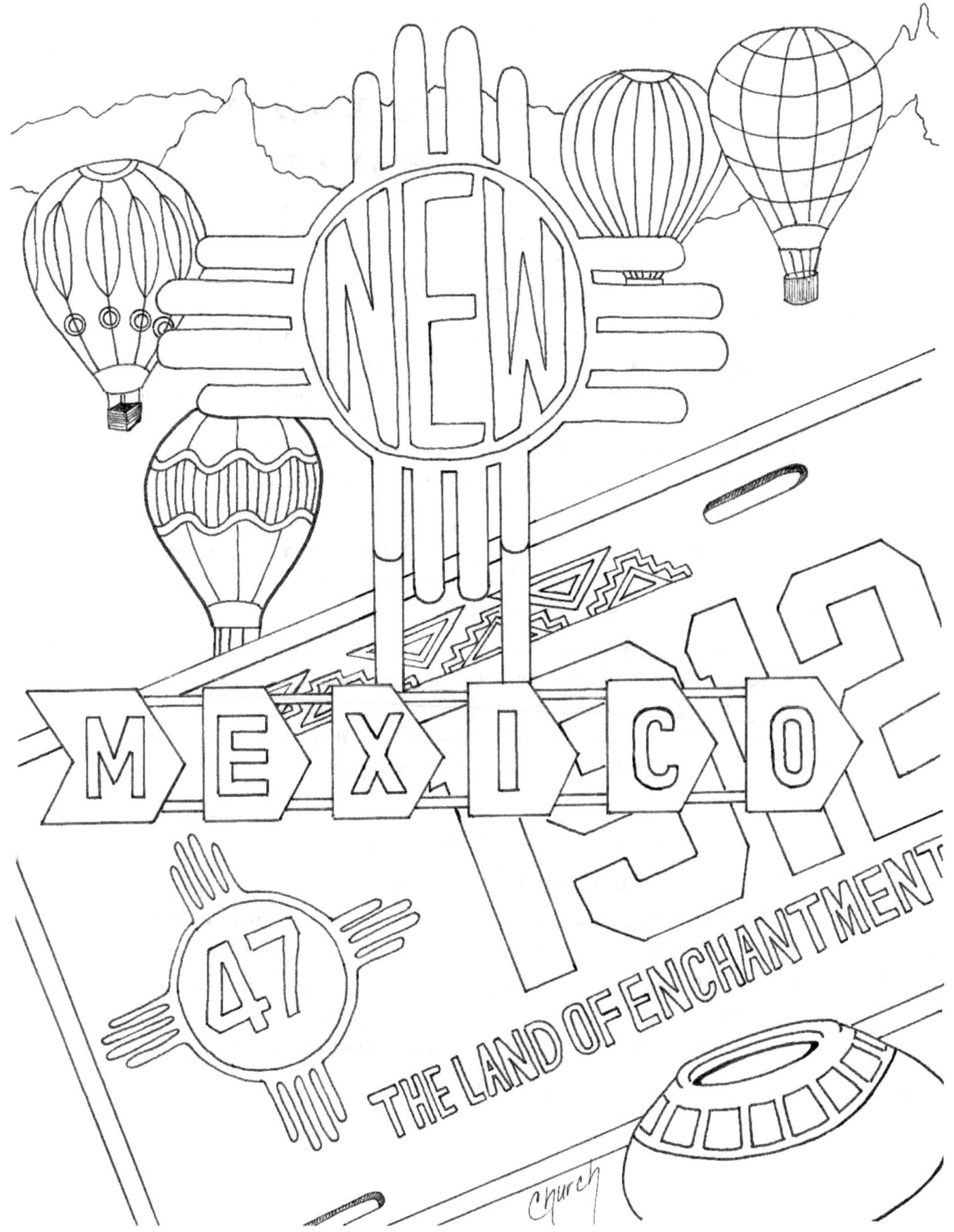

Southwest Native Americans

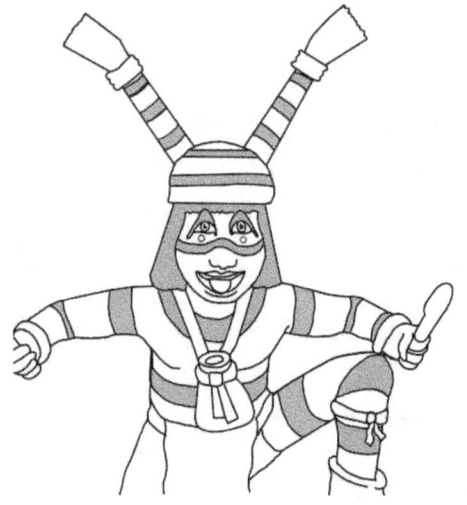

As you are traveling through New Mexico and Arizona you will see some whimsical looking dolls in the many gifts shops along the Route. These dolls are call Kachina dolls and the name carries a long history.

The Southwest Native Americans, which include tribes of New Mexico and Arizona, have inhabited the area for well over 2,000 years. The Pueblo people believed that after the winter solstice great spirits would come down from the mountains and bless their crops for a bountiful harvest. The Kachinas would walk upon the earth to interact with the Pueblo people, only return to the spirit world at the end of the planting season.

With the Hopi people, only the men could dress in a Kachina costume to perform dances and ceremonies. If the ritual was performed correctly, then the men could interact with the spiritual beings.

The dolls were created for the Kachinas and were traditionally made from a single piece of cottonwood root. They were not a doll to play with but a doll that was passed down from generation to generation, often staying with the tribe for hundreds of years. The Navajo began making their own Kachina dolls in the 20th century, adding their own decorative elements such as beads and turquoise to the dolls.

There are four basic types of Kachina dolls:

1. *Putsqatihu* – made for infants, a simple flat figure.
2. *Putstihu taywa'yla* – given to toddlers, flat body but 3 dimensional face.
3. *Murinputihu* – given to infant girls, carved into a cylinder shape.
4. *Tithu* – fully developed figures given to Hopi girls age 2 and older at ceremonies.

* All colors shown together symbolizes heaven or Zenith

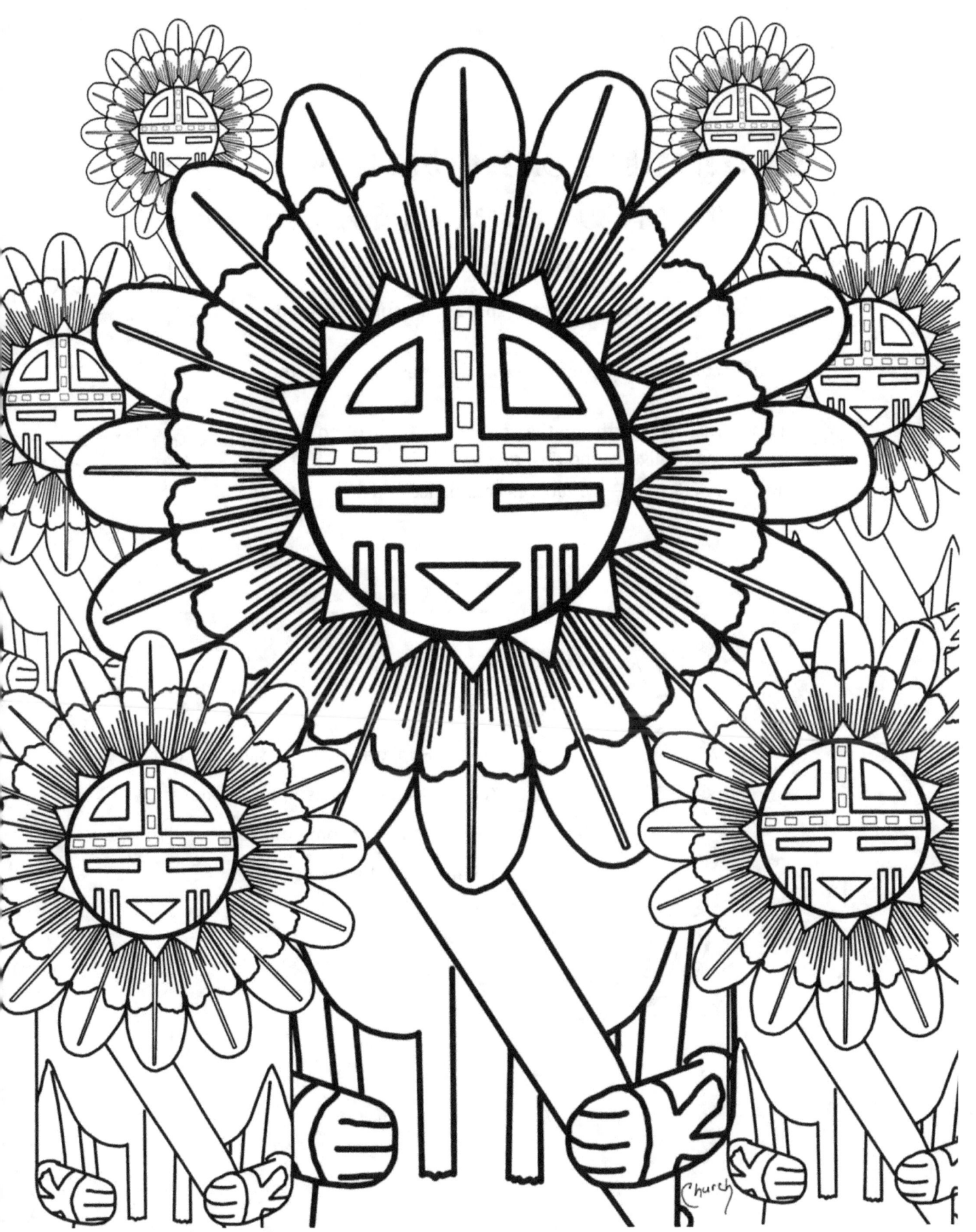

Examples of just a few of the over 400 types of Kachina dolls

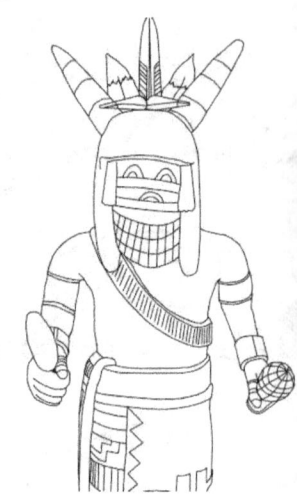

- Crow Mother – carries a basket of sprouts, a symbol of germination of seeds
- Hemis Kachina – wears a mask, fertility, carries a rattle for the sound of rain
- Masau – rules the earth and the underworld Puchkofmoktaka –aka: scorpion, comic figure who runs races
- Tawa or Sun Kachina – symbolizes abundance and life.

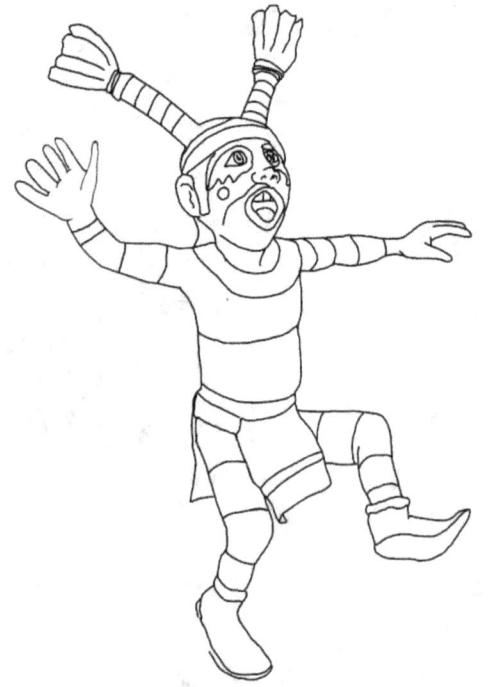

In the Hopi tradition, the Sacred Clown Kachina frequently disrupts and makes a holy mess out of some of the most vital and fundamental rituals.

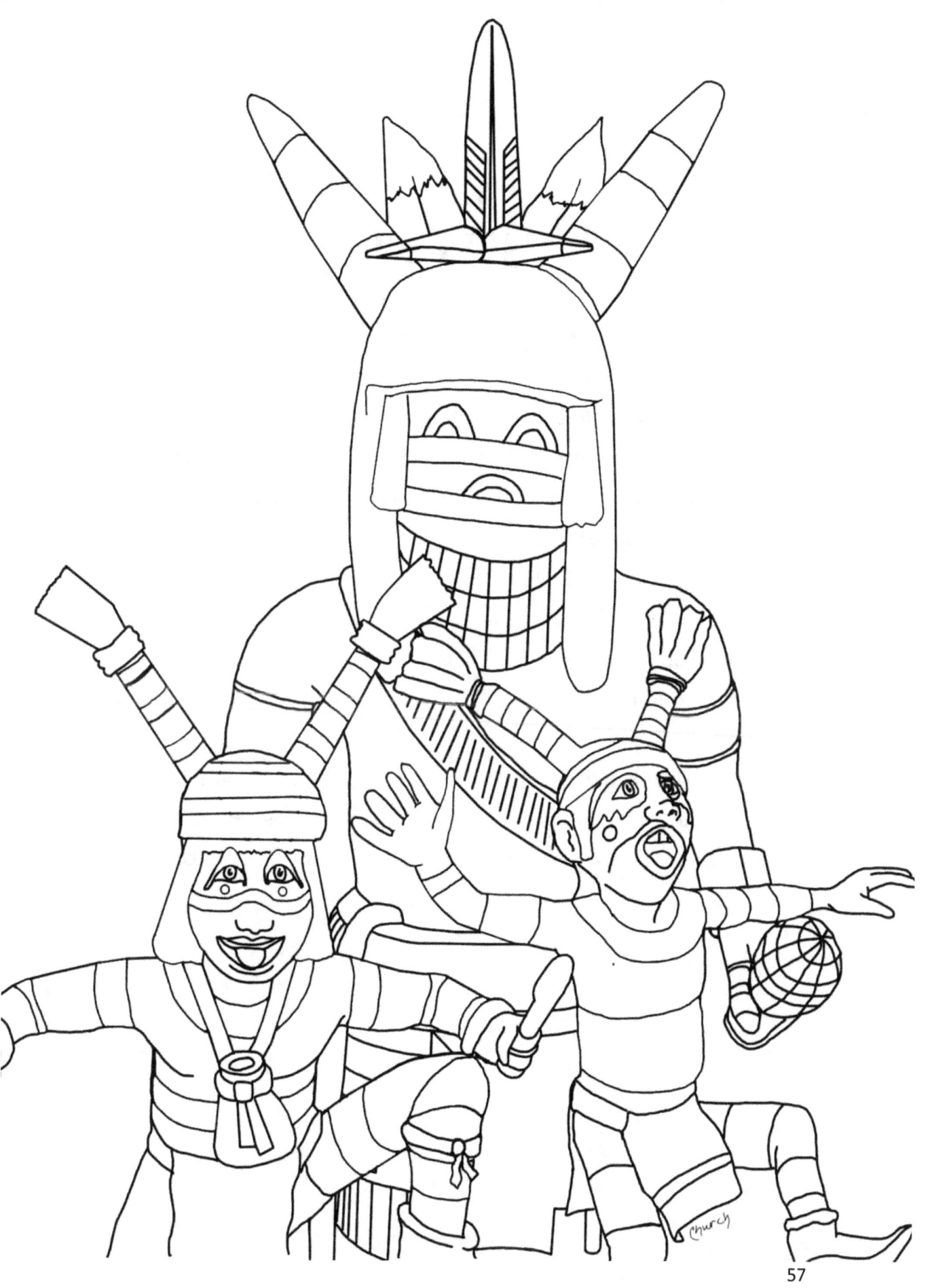

Arizona

"The Grand Canyon State"
State motto is – "Ditat Deus" meaning God Enriches

It took 22 years before Arizona was admitted into statehood on February 14, 1912, entitling Arizona with the nickname the Valentine State. Joining the Union as the 48th and the 6th largest state, the Valentine State closed the gap between New Mexico and California.

Arizona's beauty and mild winters make it especially popular for tourists, not to mention it does have one of the seven natural wonders of the world in its back yard, the Grand Canyon. The beautifully carved Grand Canyon is 277 miles long, 18 miles wide, and 1 mile deep. There are more than just canyons and tall cactus to see in Arizona; the brilliantly colored rocks and clay in the Painted Desert, the million year old fossilized trees in the Petrified Forest, and ancient Indian ruins that have been designated national monuments are just a few of the must see places. Of course, there was also the big shoot out at the O.K. Corral in Tombstone, with the Earp brothers and Doc Holliday.

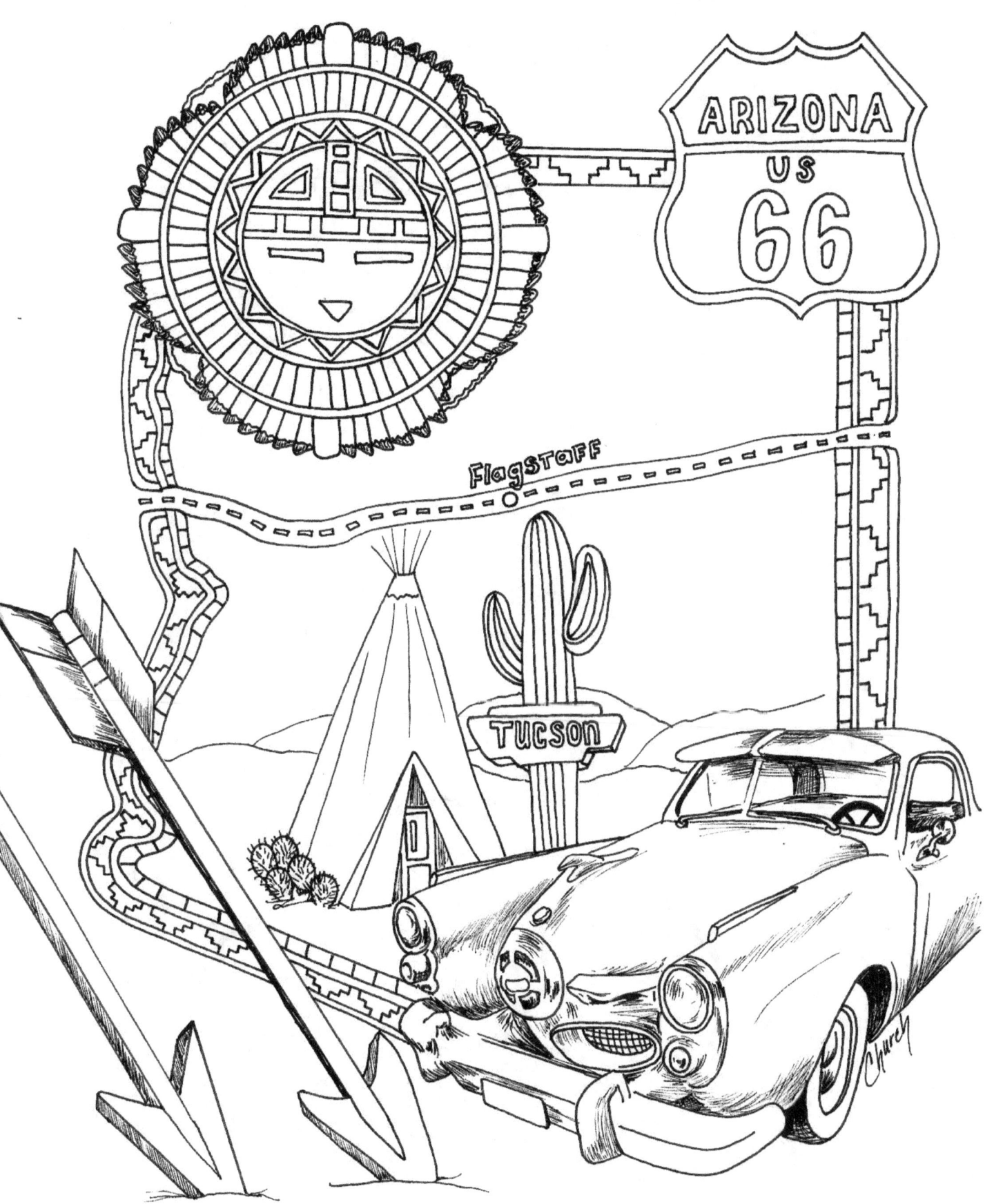

ARIZONA
US
66

Flagstaff

Tucson

Old Trails Highway

Route 66 through Arizona proved to be a treacherous route and in some aspects, the deadliest. The "Mother Road" gave way to less flattering nicknames such as the "Bloody Highway" or "Death Alley."

In 1914, the road that was to become Route 66 was designated "National Old Trails Highway." In 1926, it became Route 66. One section in the Black Mountains, just outside of an old mining town, Oatman, now a ghost town, is a maze of hairpin turns and the steepest grades throughout the entire stretch of Route 66. It is so steep and dangerous that some of the earlier travelers would not even dare to drive it. Instead, they opted to hire the locals to navigate the winding grade. This section of the road is still open for travel today but is now called Oatman Highway.

An exciting event that takes place in Arizona is the Annual Historic Route 66 Fun Run. Rain or shine, the Fun Run goes from Seligman to Kingman and attracts more than 800 cars along with thousands of spectators from around the world.

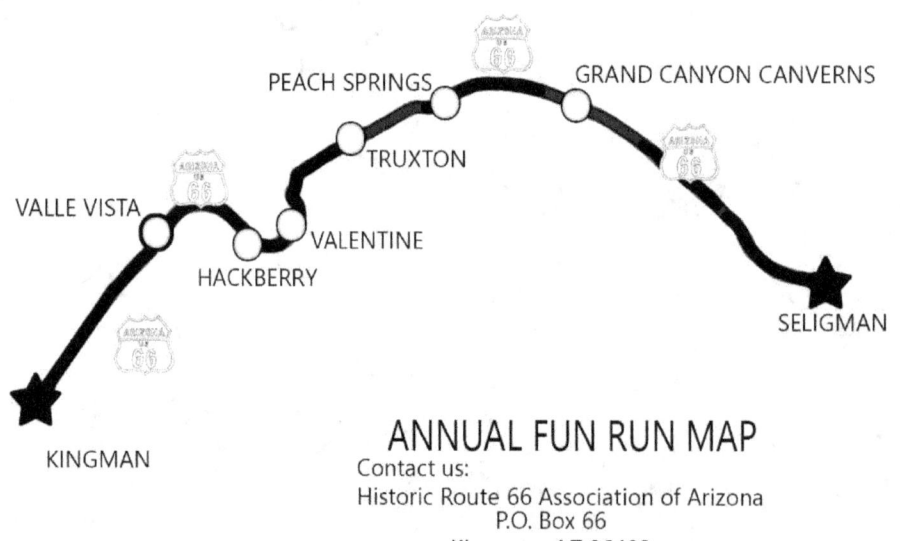

ANNUAL FUN RUN MAP
Contact us:
Historic Route 66 Association of Arizona
P.O. Box 66
Kingman, AZ 86402
Phone: (928) 753-5001   FAX: (928) 753-5852

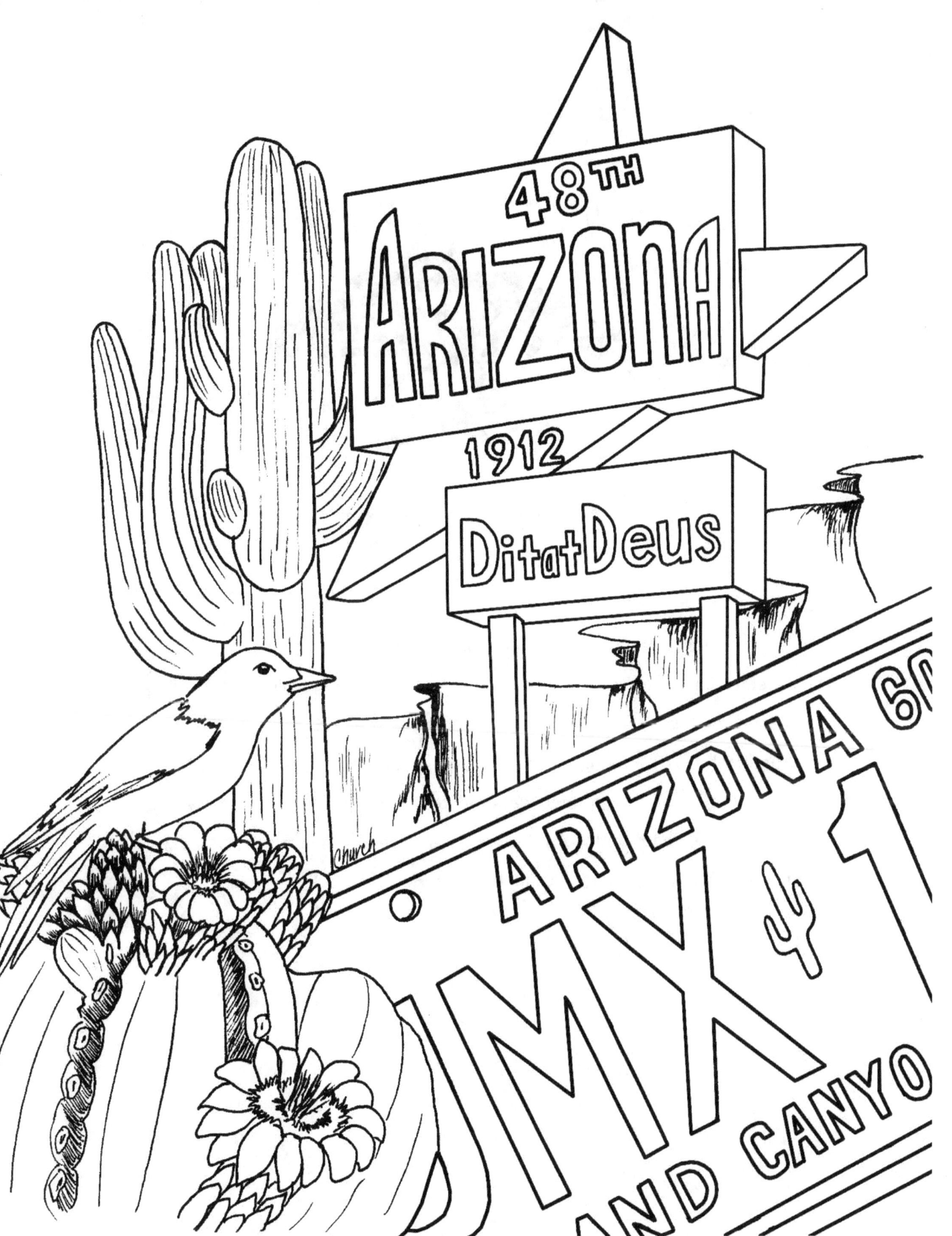

Code Talkers

After Japan bombed Pearl Harbor in 1941, the U.S. Marines needed a secret language to transmit communications. The brave Navajo Indians from Arizona enlisted and by using their native tongue, they were able to save countless lives. The young Navajo men were known as the Navajo Code Talkers. The oral code that they created was un-decipherable by the enemy, fulfilling a crucial role during World War II. There were more than 430 code talkers, "who answered the call of duty following the Pearl Harbor attacks."

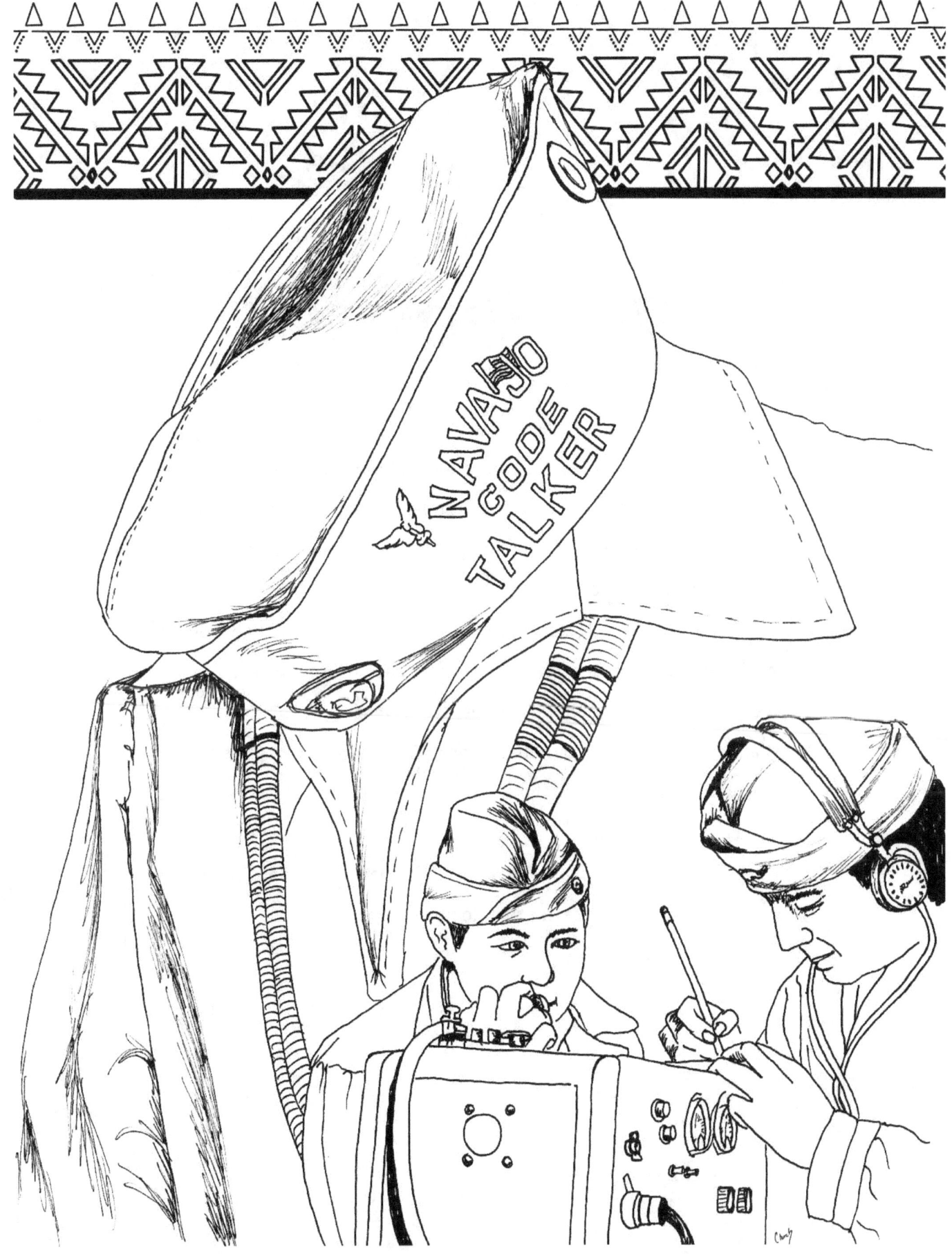

The Hottest and the Coldest

Arizona has the greatest percentage of its acreage designated as Indian tribal land in the United States. One of the oldest, continuously inhabited settlements in the United States belong to the Indian Hopi village, Oraibi, which has been in existence dating back to 1150 AD.

Arizona is the only state that can yield both the highest and lowest temperatures in the country within the same day. This type of environment makes it ideal for the state bird, Cactus Wren, which relies on the plentiful Saguaro cactus blossoms for nourishment. The beautiful blossoms spreading throughout the land became the state flower in 1931; nineteen years after Arizona became a state.

Most of the states in the U.S. recognize Daylight Savings Time, however, Arizona is one of the two states that do not.

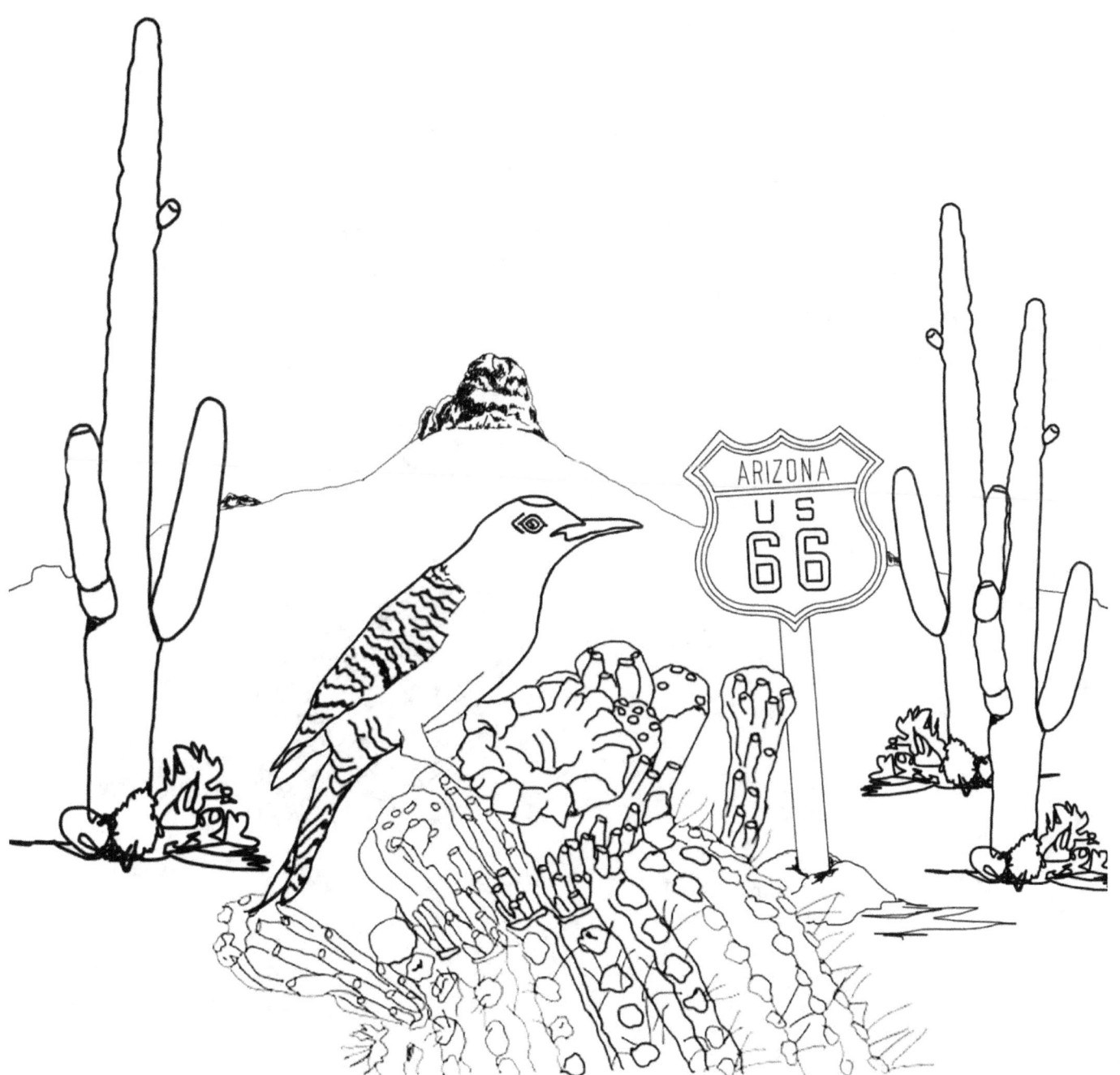

California
"The Golden State"

State flower – Golden Poppies

From the Mojave Desert, over mountains and valleys, to the beautiful beaches, "The Golden State" jumped to full statehood, after much debate over whether to allow slavery. California, the 31st state, entered the Union as a free state in 1850.

As a rule, regions had to become a formal territory before they could become a state. Once they obtained 60,000 inhabitants, they then could apply for statehood. Due to California's population almost doubling 60,000 in one year from Gold Fever, it became the only state to skip this territorial requirement. This began California's long reign as the most powerful economic and political force in the far West.

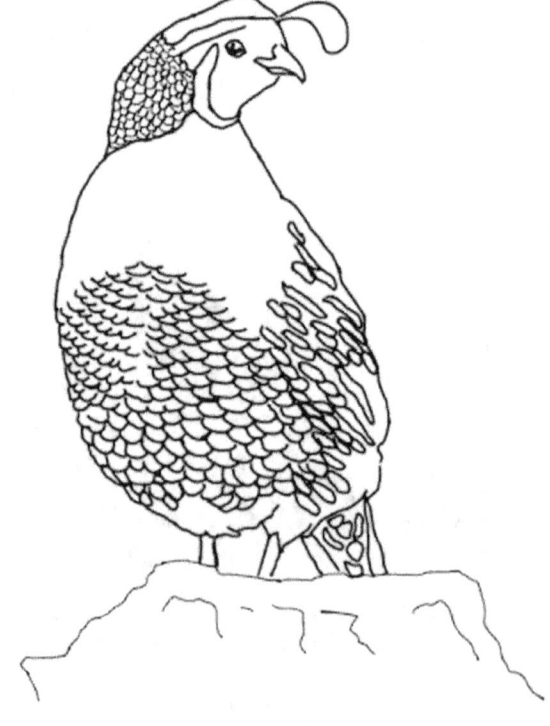

State bird – Quail

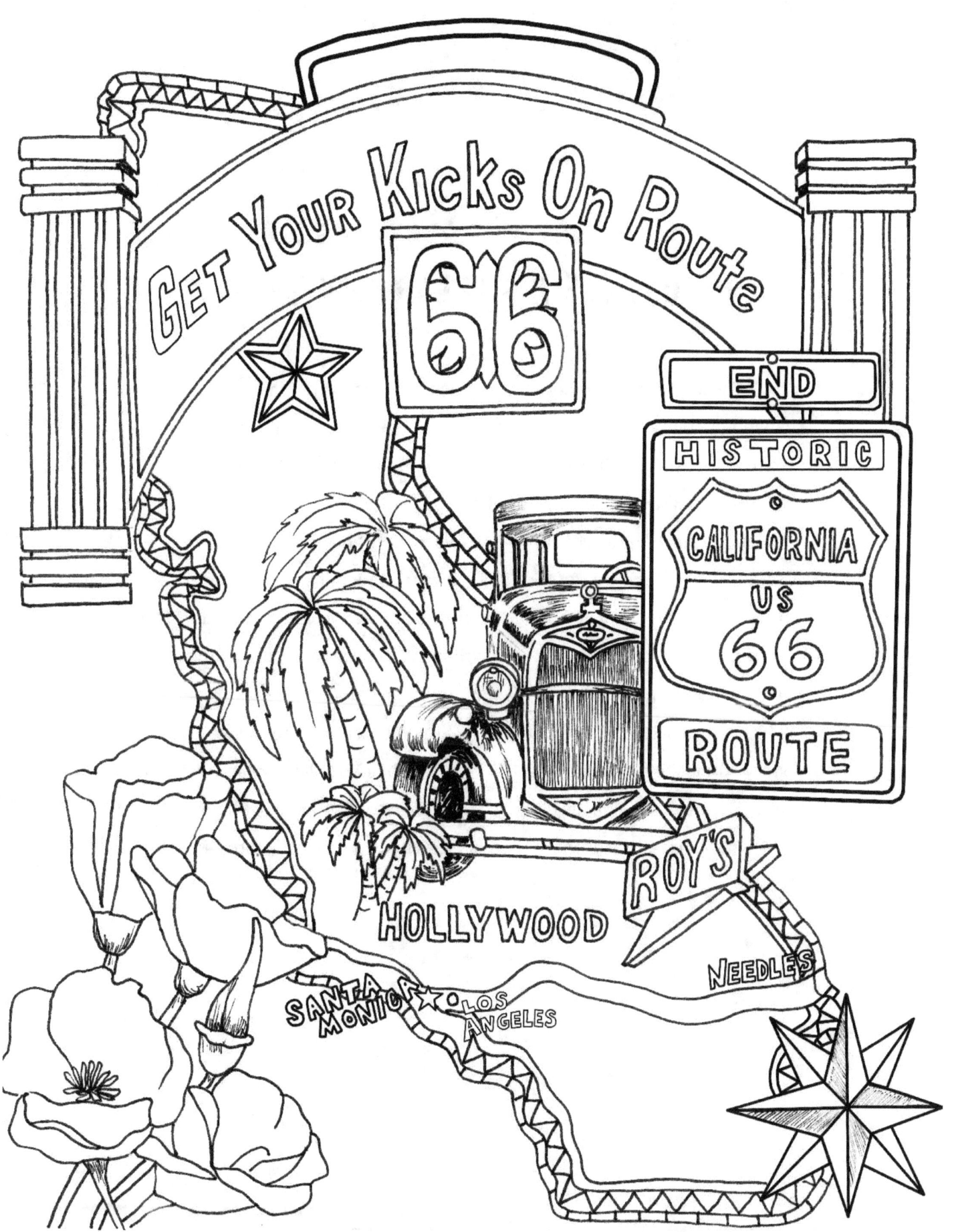

The California Gold Rush of 1849

The gold nuggets discovered in the Sacramento Valley in early 1848 changed the West Coast almost overnight. As news spread of the discovery of gold by James Wilson Marshall, a carpenter who found gold while building a water-powered sawmill, thousands of prospective gold miners traveled by sea or over land to jump on the gold fever bandwagon.   His discovery was in the American River at the base of the Sierra Nevada Mountains near Coloma, California. By the end of 1849, the non-native population of California territory was over 100,000 compared to the less than 1,000 prior to the discoveries. The miners extracted more than 750,000 pounds of gold during the Gold Rush.

The Gold Rush was one of the most significant events to shape American history during the first half of the 19th century. The two billion dollars' worth of precious metal hit its limit in 1852, but the growth of California continued. Today Los Angeles is classified as the second largest city in the United States behind New York City.

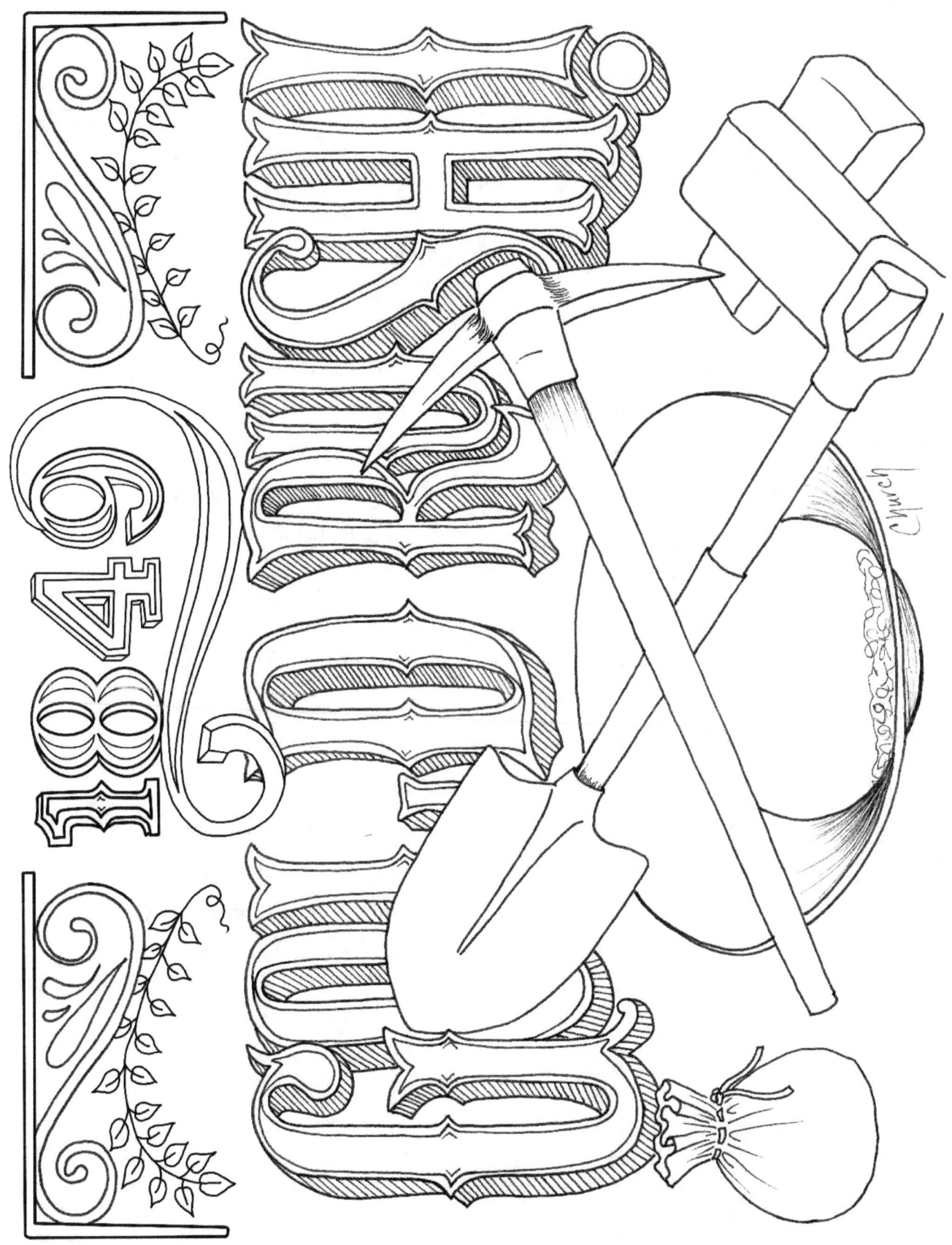

The Hottest town in the USA

Three hundred and twenty miles of a wide variety of geography and cultures, Route 66 opened up the state, making it accessible to thousands of travelers seeking the dream of prosperity and hope. The most legendary travelers of the continent were the Okies of the Great Depression, who left their memories and despair behind to enter into the promise land.

Route 66 winds through deserts, mountains, ghost towns, metropolitan areas, and even along the fearsome and feared "San Andreas Fault", the source of many geological movements. One of the towns that the road passes through is Needles, California. It is also known to be the hottest town in the United States, with temperatures often exceeding 105 degrees Fahrenheit during the summer months.

As of the ninetieth anniversary of Route 66, the three hundred and twenty miles of memorable road in California, has approximately three hundred and fifteen miles that are still intact and drivable.

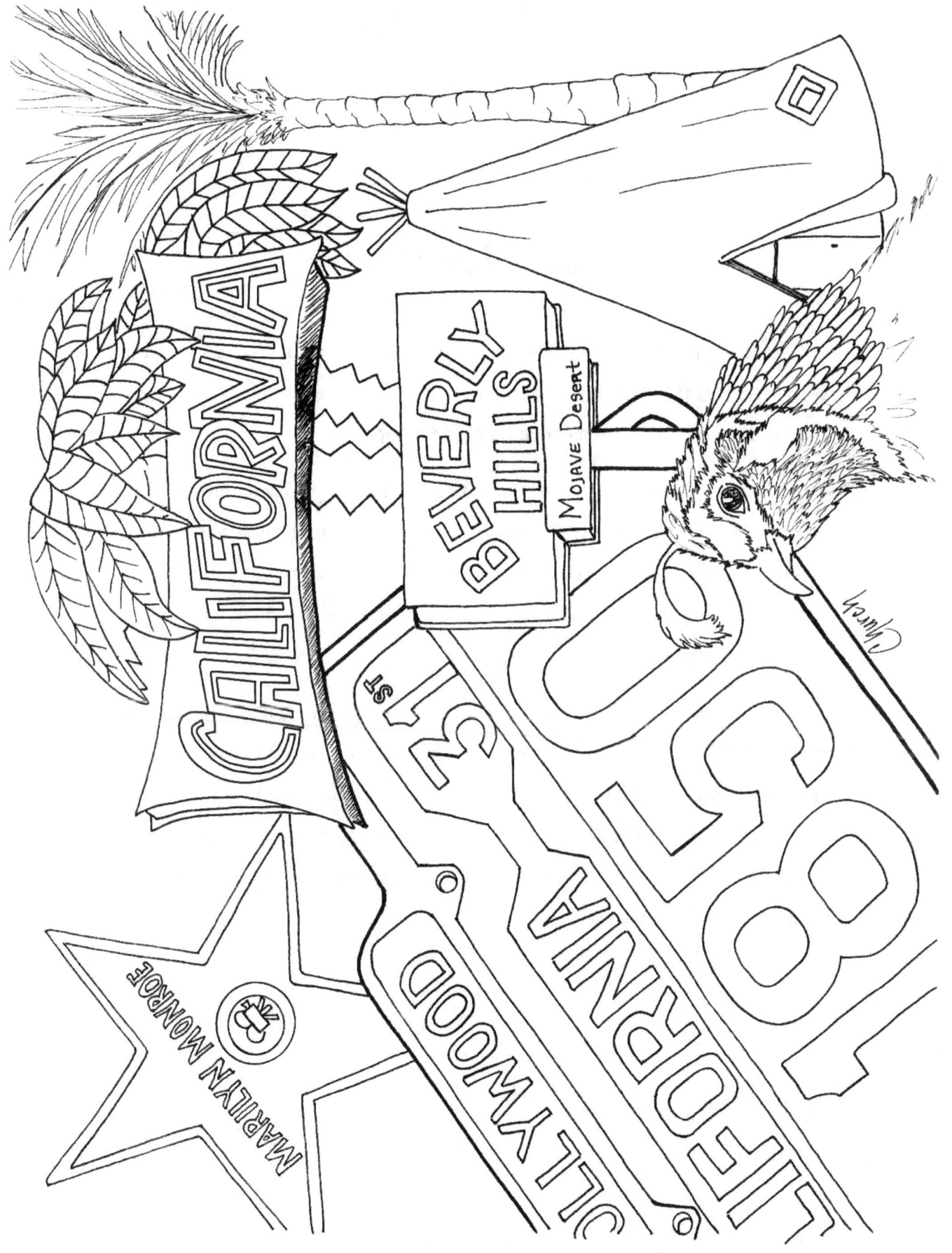

Liquid Fire

For more than 4,000 years, the use of advertising displays at businesses were the only effective advertising medium. Signs were evident in ancient Egypt and Greece, even in the ruins of Pompeii and other cities.

Neon sign technology dates back to 1675, before the age of electricity. An astronomer observed a faint glow in a mercury barometer tube when shaken, but the cause was not then understood. It was not until 1891 when the first electric neon sign was erected in New York City. The sign was 50 ft. high and 80 ft. wide and contained 1,457 bulbs.

How did they come up with the name neon? The word neon comes from the Greek "neos," meaning "the new gas." In 1923 a French company introduced neon gas signs in the United States, selling two to a dealership in Los Angeles for $24,000. Before long neon took off in popularity. It was great for outdoor advertising in the day or night. People would stop and stare at the neon signs, dubbing it "liquid fire."

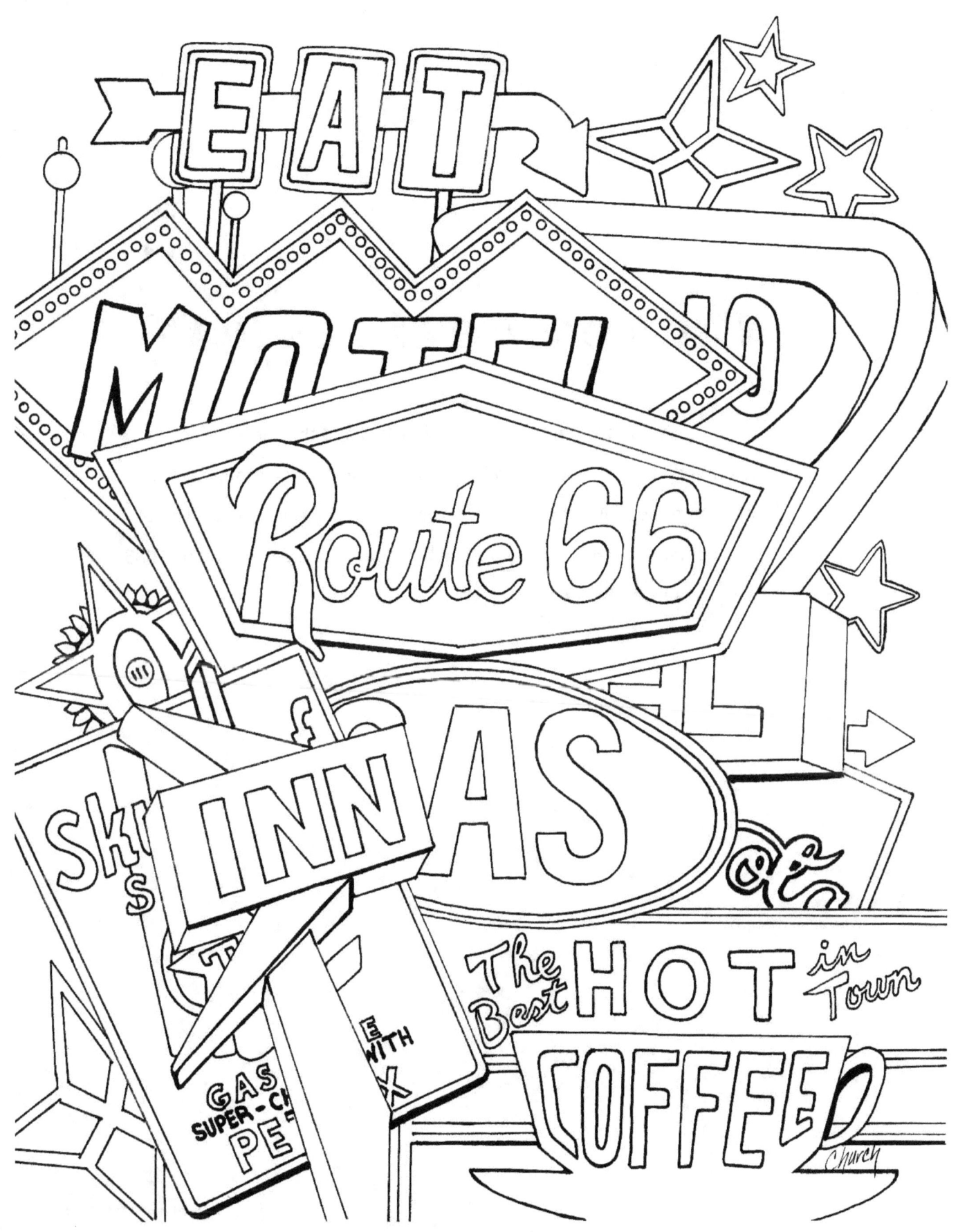

The Demise of Route 66

Excessive truck use during World War I and the comeback of the automobile industry immediately following World War II brought great pressure to bear on American highways. By 1970 nearly all segments of the original Route 66 were by-passed by a four lane highway and by 1985 all signs marking the great road were taken down.

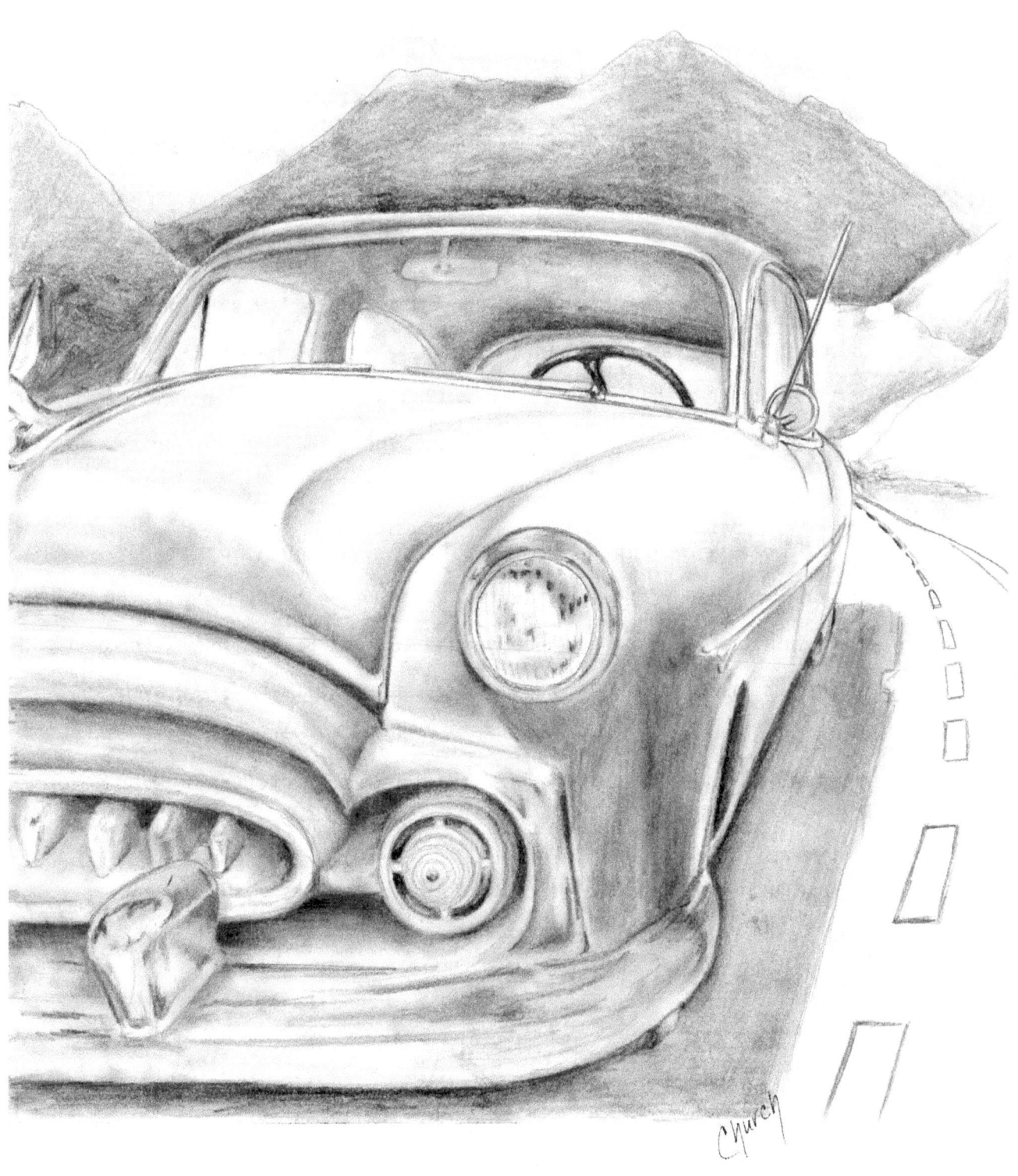

The Effects of President Ike

In 1956, President Eisenhower signed the Federal-Aid Highway Act, which assembled America's Interstate Highway System, replacing the longer routes that stopped at all of the towns. Interstate 40 soon replaced a large portion of the beloved Route 66. Sadly, by 1985, Route 66 had been removed from the United States Highway system, putting the familiar highway markers to rest.

Today the memories of this historic pathway continue with the variety of non-profit groups that have formed to help preserve the historic highway. The road was not just a main driveline between Chicago and Santa Monica; it was a road of dreams, adventures, and desperados. Because of their effort, travelers continue driving on the remaining segments of Route 66, starting a new era and leading to the once retired signs going back up. Thousands of adventurers from all over the world enjoy these vintage peeks of the past along the old highway.

Even though officially Route 66 no longer exists, there is still a great deal of it remaining to be driven by travelers far and near.

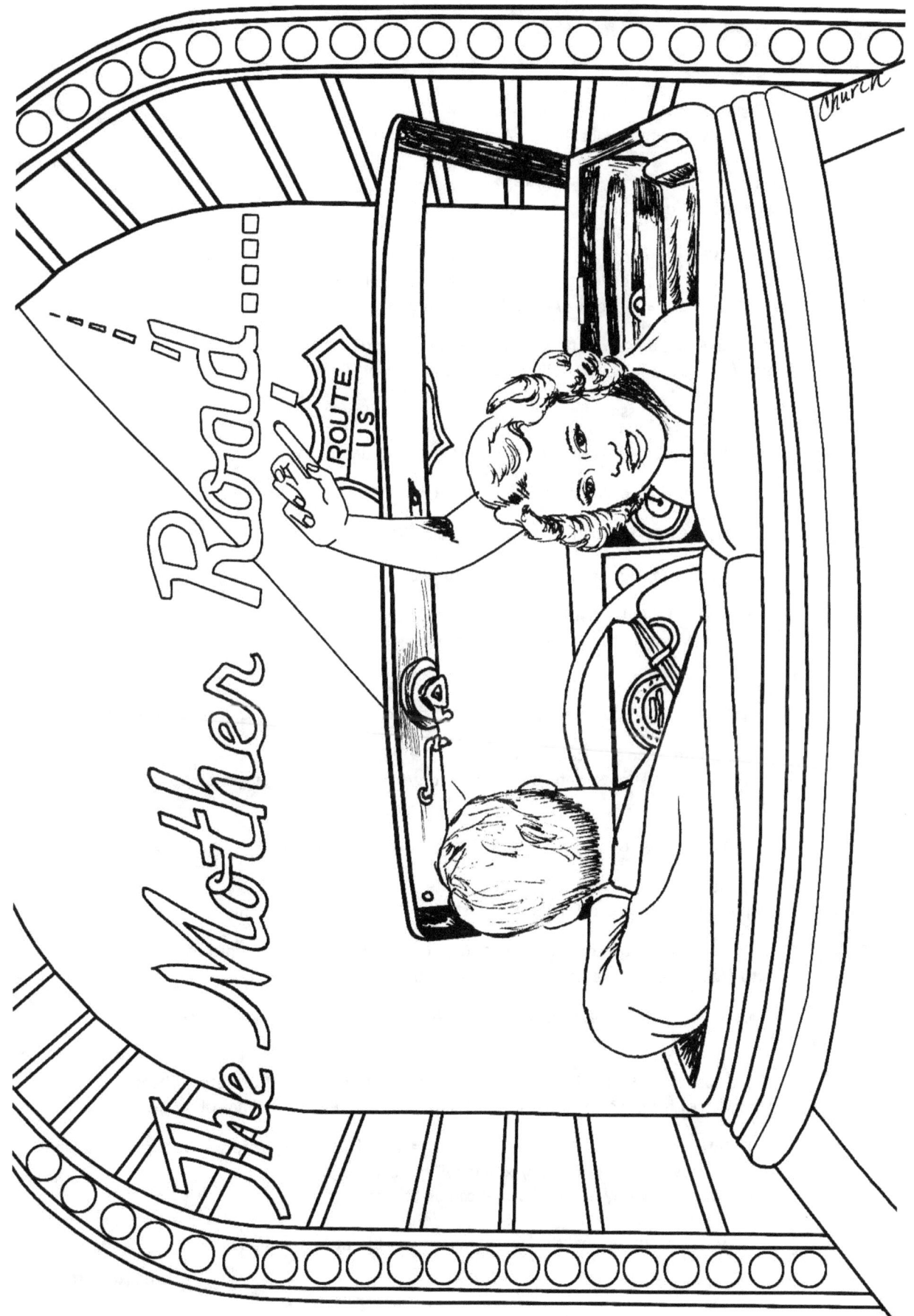

Resources:

Pulaski County Tourism Bureau.
http://www.visitpulaskicounty.org/trail_of_tears.asp

The Legend of the Cherokee rose - Powersource.,
www.powersource.com/cocinc/articles/rose.htm

Native Words Native Warriors. Smithsonian National Museum of the American Indian.
http://www.nmai.si.edu/education/codetalkers/html/ Illinois
Route 66 Association. http://www.il66assoc.org/

Missouri Route 66 Association. http://missouri66.org/?p=1323.,
http://missouri66.org/?p=1323., http://missouri66.org/?page_id=699

Kansas Route 66 Association. http://kshistoricroute66.com/

Oklahoma Route 66 Association. http://oklahomaroute66.com/

Texas Route 66 Association. http://rt66oftexas.com/

Arizona Route 66 Association., http://azrt66.com/

California Route 66 Association., http://route66ca.org/

The History of Hood Ornaments. Discount Hood Ornaments. Powered by Build A Niche Store.,
http://www.discounthoodornaments.com/history

The History and Collectability of Gas Pumps
 http://www.automobiledrivingmuseum.org/the-history-and-collectability-of-gaspumps/

First Gas Pump and Service Station
American Oil and Gas Society. http://aoghs.org/transportation/first-gas-pumpand-service-stations/

National Historical Route 66 Federation. http://national66.org/history-of-route66/

Crapanzano, C. (2010) A brief history of route 66.
http://content.time.com/time/nation/article/0,8599,2000095,00.html

Weiser, Kathy. (2016) Legendary Route 66, Route 66 Information and history.
http://www.legendsofamerica.com/66-info.html

Jensen, J. Road Trip USA. Cross country adventures on America's two-lane highways.
https://roadtripusa.com/route-66/

Nix, Elizabeth (2016) 8 things you may not know about route 66. The History Channel.
http://www.history.com/news/history-lists/8-things-you-may-not-knowabout-route-66

The Mother Road, Route 66. http://www.route66world.com/66_history/ Will Rogers Biography,
Bio. http://www.biography.com/people/will-rogers-40870
The People's Highway Route 66, American on the move.
http://amhistory.si.edu/onthemove/exhibition/exhibition_10_3.htm "Life doesn't happen along
the interstates. It's against the law." —William Least Heat Moon, Blue Highways

Traveling the Mother Road has been a life-changing event for me. To truly see and do everything there is to do you need about three to four weeks and you still will not be able to do and see everything. I visited with a man who told me that he has been traveling the road since 1959. He was a tour guide for the Route for several years and even today, he still has new experiences. The Road does not have to be rushed and experienced in just one get away, it could be broken up into states, which is what I did. I even broke the state up into several excursions. I realized that there is so much involved with the ever-evolving Route 66 that I could not possibly get it all in one book or even make a half way attempt. I have continued my series of Route 66 into individual states breaking it down to counties. Each edition will have more detailed destinations listed, photo opportunities, landmarks, some still there and some that are gone and amazing eateries. These state-by-state books are in an Art Deco style honoring the vintage 20's and 30's automobiles and architecture. You will also find a map to guide you through Route 66 complements of each states Route 66 Association. And plus, the big bonus is more exciting and fun coloring pages. These books could be your Route 66 passports, or journals of your trip. You can add stamps, stickers, postcards or even photos to the pages. The skies the limit and it is your journey enjoy it to its fullest.

The state series books will be coming available throughout 2017 and 2018. Front covers of all nine books are watercolor originals by myself that I have created from various vintage cars and trucks that people have let me paint. Prints are available and can be viewed on my website cherylchurch.com shipping is available.

Collect all 9 books.

> The Perfect Escape, Illinois Adventure on Route 66
> The Perfect Escape, Missouri Adventure on Route 66
> The Perfect Escape, Kansas Adventure on Route 66
> The Perfect Escape, Oklahoma Adventure on Route 66
> The Perfect Escape, Texas Adventure on Route 66
> The Perfect Escape, New Mexico Adventure on Route 66
> The Perfect Escape, Arizona Adventure on Route 66
> The Perfect Escape, California Adventure on Route 66

As always.........Happy Coloring!